Judy Klipin was born in Johannesburg, South Africa, where she continues to live with her family. Judy specialises in working with people who are experiencing burnout and people who had challenging childhoods (adult children); more often than not these are the same people. She runs an Adult Child Coach Apprenticeship programme for coaches who want to work in this field.

Judy combines her knowledge and skills as a Martha Beck Certified Master Life Coach and a Transactional Analysis practitioner to teach her clients simple, practical and powerful tools that help them to change – not who they are, but how they are. She coaches, mentors and trains individuals and groups, both in person and through phone and internet coaching.

Judy has a BA and HDipED from the University of the Witwatersrand and a Masters in Social Sciences from Leicester University.

Judy is also the author of *Recover from your Childhood: Life Lessons for the Adult Child*.

Find out more at www.judyklipin.com

For Stephen

Recover from Burnout

Life lessons to regain your passion and purpose

Judy Klipin

BOOK**STORM**

ISBN: 978-1-928257-60-8
e-ISBN: 978-1-928257-61-5

First edition, first impression 2019

Published by Bookstorm (Pty) Ltd
PO Box 4532
Northcliff 2115
Johannesburg
South Africa
www.bookstorm.co.za

Edited by Tracey Hawthorne
Proofread by Wesley Thompson
Cover design by mr design
Book design and layout by René de Wet
Printed and bound by Pinetown Printers

Contents

Introduction

What is burnout?

Burnout is a result of doing too many of the wrong things.

In my 12-year career as a life coach I've seen burnout in many and varied clients. There are the high-powered executives (men and women) who are so tired and stressed that the only things keeping them going are the caffeine, cigarettes and high-carb foods with which they're fuelling their exhausted bodies. There are the tearful and vulnerable women who are so drained by the demands of family, friends and work that they have no energy left over to spend on looking after themselves. There are the angry and resentful men who try to drown their disappointment and disillusionment in alcohol. Almost every one of my clients who works in the public sector shows signs of burnout, from stressed and traumatised police officers, to exhausted and overwhelmed senior managers, to anxious and disengaged workers. Men and women from all walks of life are vulnerable to burnout.

I believe that we get burnout from deceiving/forcing/cajoling ourselves into doing things that are wrong for us. We get burnout because we have leaky boundaries: we let people in instead of keeping them out; we say yes when we should say no; we go places, do things and see people that not only don't spark joy, but actually evoke despair.

Doing what we don't want to or feel uncomfortable doing burns up more energy than we get back. It doesn't matter if it's little (answering a phonecall from someone who drains us) or large (staying in a job that we hate or that's at odds with our personal value system), every time we force ourselves to do something that feels wrong to us, we're using up far more energy than we're getting back. And if we're losing energy rather than generating it – or at the very least breaking even – we will get burnout. The rate of energy loss determines the speed and severity with which we develop the burnout.

It isn't just that our energy is drained by unrewarding mental, physical and emotional effort. The resentment, anxiety, frustration and stress that accompany doing things that are wrong for us result in floods of harmful and even toxic chemicals being released into our bodies. The noxious combination of energy deficit and stress-hormone cocktail leads to physical, emotional and mental weakness and disease that can end up as a whole range of serious conditions. Burnout left unaddressed progresses and can lead to full-blown depression, diabetes and even heart disease – not to mention divorce, disillusionment and dread!

There are many flavours of burnout. There's the need-a-caffeine-fix-to-get-you-going-in-the-morning burnout that has you eating everything containing caffeine, sugar, carbs or salt that you can lay your hands on. There's combative burnout, which makes you pick a fight with everyone – family, friends, colleagues, strangers in traffic… There's the not-wanting-to-talk-to-anyone-or-do-anything (other than lie in bed and watch undemanding movies or read trashy novels) burnout. There's the miserable, depressed and dispirited burnout that makes you question every life choice you've ever made. There's the burnout that has you so bone weary and so depleted that you can't even pull a door closed, let alone yourself towards yourself. And there are many others too.

When I first started telling people about my burnout work I was met with a variety of responses: 'There's no such thing as burnout' (from a specialist physician); 'I've noticed that people who exercise regularly don't seem to get burnout' (from an emergency-room doctor); 'Poor people can't afford to have burnout'; 'It's just middle-class laziness and self-indulgence'.

For quite some time I felt like an almost lone voice in the wilderness, speaking up about something I saw to be a serious and chronic health issue. Now, at last, burnout is becoming increasingly recognised. I suspect it's because we just can't ignore any longer how exhausted, overwhelmed and depleted we are as individuals and collectively.

Burnout is a real thing and it's a real, and growing, problem. Finally, it's being acknowledged and taken seriously. More and more people are talking about it, reading about it and acting on it. Thankfully, there is a much greater awareness and acceptance of burnout as a genuine condition.

Burnout is an epidemic

Burnout has long been associated with overworked and stressed corporate high-flyers, but it's becoming increasingly apparent that it's a condition that spreads its reach far and wide. Burnout has moved out of the boardroom and is present in every nook and cranny of our society.

A couple of years ago I was invited to discuss burnout with the host of a late-night radio show that gets broadcast to the whole of my home city, Johannesburg. Jozi is South Africa's biggest city and the capital of the richest province in the country. It's recognised as the economic powerhouse of the country and the region. Joburgers are proud of the fact that we work hard and play hard in a city that's always busy and bustling.

I'm never surprised by the number of people who listen to and call in on late-night radio, but the range and content of the many, many calls and text messages was a little startling. They served to confirm for me something that I'd long suspected: burnout is an epidemic. Men and women, young and old, from all walks of life, were calling in to share their stories and ask questions. Housewives, students, young adults in their first jobs, executive businesspeople, teachers, mothers, doctors, nurses, police officers, social workers, journalists… all were complaining of feeling run down, exhausted and overwhelmed by life in general and their lives in particular.

For a long while I wondered if the high incidence of burnout was a South African thing. There's no doubt that South Africans have a very particular and peculiar relationship with stress, anxiety and fear. For as long as any of us can remember, we've lived in a country and within a society that's unpredictable and inconsistent. We've experienced change and uncertainty, distress about the past, and fear for the future, and no small degree of political and social instability. I think it's fair to say South Africans are burnout overachievers!

That said, the more aware and attuned I became to all things burnout, the more I saw evidence of it farther afield. Social media is filled with discussions about burnout. LinkedIn and other professional networking sites feature articles on burnout by the likes of businesswoman Arianna Huffington, research professor Brené Brown and entrepreneur Richard Branson. If you type 'burnout' into any search engine, millions of results come up.

WHAT'S THE DIFFERENCE BETWEEN BURNOUT AND DEPRESSION?
On that radio show, what I found to be very concerning was the number of callers who seemed to have tipped over from burnout and into depression. Because burnout and depression look very similar, it can be difficult to differentiate between the two. I've been diagnosed with depression when I thought I had burnout, and with burnout when I thought I had depression. When the lines are blurred it takes a very skilled and experienced professional to differentiate between the two conditions.

Burnout and depression can both show themselves through changes in eating and sleeping patterns, irritability, social withdrawal, loss of interest in things that used to feel significant, feelings of worthlessness and hopelessness, difficulty concentrating and – perhaps most obviously – a deep and abiding exhaustion.

It's the *nature* of the exhaustion that helps to discern between burnout and depression. I believe that depression is a feeling of being tired *of* life whereas burnout is a feeling of being tired *from* life. I can't stress enough, however, how important it is to seek professional help in getting the correct diagnosis and support for whichever condition you're experiencing.

In my view, burnout evolves into depression when we ignore and ignore and ignore our exhaustion and our body and its pleas for help and change until eventually our spirit starts to give up hope. And having to deal with depression on top of burnout is a double whammy that I wouldn't wish on anyone.

The aims of this book

Burnout isn't one thing. It's a complex condition that arises from a whole series of beliefs, choices and actions that we consciously or unconsciously feel and take. Getting to the bottom of it requires a level of energy and motivation that many people don't have while in the grips of the exhaustion.

My aim with this book is to support you to regain your energy and enthusiasm in order to help you to reconnect with your purpose, passion and productivity. Each chapter will help you to start implementing ideas and practices to do just that.

The book has two parts. Part I is designed to help you regain your energy and enthusiasm by providing practical ideas and tools, while Part II takes you on a deeper journey of understanding yourself and your fears and beliefs so that you'll be able to make profound changes and maintain your gusto and strength. Interspersed throughout the book are pages that are designed to help you pause – to stop and come back to yourself before continuing with the reading journey.

It's time to allow yourself to thrive

This book will provide you with a set of concepts and tools that may challenge you at the same time as they support you. The tasks and tools will help you to reach a deeper understanding of why you've been dancing with burnout, and enable you to take the good and leave the bad behind. All of the insights and 'aha' or lightbulb moments should help you to recognise that the behaviours that lead to burnout aren't all bad. You and your Survivor Self have developed many creative, resourceful and innovative responses to life and all its challenges. There's much to appreciate and be grateful for.

But without a deep understanding there can be no change. And without change, burnout will be a regular visitor in your life. The journey you're about to embark on is designed to support you to bring your creative responses and your health and wellbeing together into a harmonious relationship.

The aim is for you to:
* Change what you can and accept what you can't change.
* Stop making a victim of yourself in your quest to save others.
* Stop sabotaging yourself and reduce the need to rescue yourself from the wrong things you have committed to.
* Pay attention to the small things, as they point to bigger things.
* Update your creative responses so that they serve you rather than exhaust you.
* Actively (and proactively) choose how you want to be in the world, in your relationships, and at your work.
* Spend your energy wisely.
* Embrace your resilience and celebrate your strength and resourcefulness.

We tend to think that big resolutions ('I'm going to stop eating sugar! I'm going to get a new job! I'm going to run away and join the circus!') are required for big changes. But remember that enormous oil tankers are turned around by making many tiny adjustments to their rudders. Every day we're faced with myriad choices. And each tiny choice we make is what turns our lives around – in a sustained way.

Let's get started!

AN APPLE A DAY...

When we feel as though we're running on empty, our mind tells us we need coffee or chocolate or a muffin – or, best yet, a chocolate muffin and a cappuccino. 'If you feed me caffeine and carbs you will have more energy,' it promises.

Your mind is a liar.

All that happens when you choose caffeine and carbs over real food is a short-lived sugar rush followed by an energy slump that will cause you to reach for another fix. Too much sugar and caffeine can result in too much of the stress hormone cortisol, which results in anxiety, stress and tummy fat – none of which is a good look or feel.

Make eating good foods easy by filling the fridge and your lunchbox with easy-to-eat nuts, fresh fruit and veggies so you're ready for snack-attacks.

REGAIN YOUR ENERGY

1

Understanding burnout

On the surface it would appear to be very bad that there's so much burnout in the world, but I think it's also partly very good, because – as Maya Angelou said – when we know better, we can do better. And I think it's very safe to say that most of us now know better.

We now know that burnout is a systemic condition that affects every element of our lives (our body, our mind, our emotions, our spirit and our relationships). We now know that if we don't take it seriously and address it, burnout can lead to all sorts of horrors, including diabetes, heart disease, depression, divorce and more. And we also now know that there are a whole lot of things that we can do to address burnout.

We can:
* ☀ Reduce stress
* ☀ Stop worrying so much
* ☀ Do more things that feel meaningful
* ☀ Improve work/life balance
* ☀ Build better boundaries
* ☀ Eat less
* ☀ Drink less
* ☀ Smoke less
* ☀ Move more
* ☀ Relax more
* ☀ Sleep more
* ☀ Learn to meditate
* ☀ Take up yoga
* ☀ See more friends

All of these suggestions have enormous merit.

But!

I don't believe that an instruction to reduce stress levels, for example, is helpful or even particularly realistic. If we knew how to stop being stressed, we would. The problem isn't that we're unaware that stress is bad for us. The problem, I believe, is that we don't know why we allow ourselves to reach stratospheric levels of stress. We don't understand what's making us unable to resist or – even more troubling – what makes us open ourselves up to those stressors.

We can take a whole lot of steps to make our lifestyle healthier, but unless we understand what needs to change in our hearts and minds, we will never effectively prevent burnout from happening to us again. We need to understand the thoughts, beliefs and fears that cause us to work ourselves to the point of overwhelming stress and exhaustion. We need to explore the reasons we feel we can't say no and can't ask for help. We need to find out what drives us to push our bodies, minds and spirits to breaking point.

Burnout and the adult child

A few years ago I wrote a book called *Life Lessons for the Adult Child* (recently republished as *Recover from your Childhood: Life Lessons for the Adult Child*). My definition of an adult child is anyone who had a childhood that was inconsistent or unpredictable in some way or for some time. This could be due to having had a parent who was an alcoholic or addict, having had a sibling or parent with a chronic or serious illness (including mental illnesses), having been sent to boarding school, having lived in an atmosphere of social, political or economic turmoil... In fact, I firmly believe that we all have at least some of the characteristics of the adult child because, even if we had a very stable and predictable childhood, the world at large is a pretty unpredictable place to be.

Through my work, I came to realise that there are many, many adult children in the world. Then I started to become aware that many of my clients were experiencing burnout. Interesting. There seemed to be a strong correlation between adult children and burnout. Coincidence? I think not. It's evident to me that many of the characteristics, beliefs and behaviours that we adult children devise and develop not only make us vulnerable to burnout but actively invite it into our lives.

This doesn't mean that all (or only) adult children will get burnout. I believe that every single one of us is vulnerable to developing burnout if we do too many of the wrong things. All of us do some things that are wrong for us some of the time, but those of us who are likely to get burnout tend to, often unknowingly, do lots of things that are wrong for us a lot of the time. Those of us who feel a deep and abiding need to look after others, to right wrongs, to support those less fortunate than ourselves, to make a difference to the world – we're all at risk of burning out. People who are drawn to the helping professions – doctors, nurses, psychologists, coaches, social workers, teachers, police officers, journalists – and those who have a sense of obligation to others – including parents and caregivers – have the potential to burn out if they aren't mindful about meeting their own needs. Adult children tend to tick many of these boxes.

The psychologist Janet Woititz, who coined the concept 'adult child', described some characteristics that are common to many adult children – and to those of us who are at risk of developing burnout. Even if you aren't an adult child, I'm pretty sure that some of these nine characteristics or behaviours will sound familiar to you. Many of them predispose us to burnout because they encourage us to override our natural ability to regulate our energy and look after ourselves properly.

1. WE GUESS WHAT 'NORMAL' IS

Do you ever feel as though everyone else has read, memorised and is able to effortlessly apply the instruction manual to life and you haven't even received it? What many of us don't realise is that not only is there no such thing as 'normal', but almost everyone feels at sea in various circumstances. There's a fantasy that all those 'theys' know how to dress, how to behave and how to regulate themselves in every situation. They know what to expect and what's expected of them. We're the only ones who feel anxious or uncomfortable in unfamiliar situations.

Guessing what normal is doesn't only cause stress and anxiety, it also means that we struggle to discern what reasonable expectations are and aren't. Is it 'normal' to have to work 12-hour days? Is it 'normal' to take work home and put in an additional four hours after supper? Is it 'normal' to find new tasks difficult? And do I have to do them all by myself or can I ask for help? Is it 'normal' to miss out on important family events because of my boss's demands? Is it okay to want to spend time doing what makes me happy instead of what makes everyone else happy?

When we don't have a clear sense of what 'normal' is, it's hard for us to assess what to say 'yes' to and what to say 'no' to. We feel we need to do what we see everyone else doing (or what we think we see everyone else doing). If we're in an environment that encourages overwork and stress, then that's what we think is normal and we go along with it. If we see blurred boundaries and erosion of principles and ideals, we think that's normal and we go along with it.

2. WE LIE WHEN IT WOULD BE JUST AS EASY TO TELL THE TRUTH

All of us lie from time to time, but some of us lie when it's just as easy to tell the truth. These are usually face-saving lies – lies we tell to make ourselves look better – like pretending to be able to do something we can't, or signing up for a task at work for which we don't have the skills or experience, but we don't want to admit this in case our boss and/or colleagues think we aren't good enough. Then we pretend to be fine and not need any help even when it's obvious to everyone around us that we do need it.

These petty lies also take the form of pretending to like something (scary movies, bungee jumping, marathon running) that we actually hate, in order to keep a friend or partner happy. Or lying to ourselves about how tired we are by telling ourselves that we have to work harder even when we're totally exhausted. Or persuading ourselves into going to a loud and crowded club even when we have a headache.

We might tell ourselves that our work isn't so bad even when we feel desperate and depressed every Sunday night. We may assure ourselves that we love the person we're with even though we need to take anti-anxiety pills in order to be in the same room as them. We could keep going to a yoga/pottery/art class even though it makes us feel incompetent and not good enough.

We're also excellent at lying by omission, when we don't ask for help, or when we pretend everything is fine when it isn't, or when we don't speak up about something that's troubling or upsetting us.

We lie to ourselves about many things – jobs, relationships, hobbies, health – and when we do, we find ourselves doing things that are wrong for us and that, eventually and inevitably, lead to burnout.

3. WE JUDGE OURSELVES WITHOUT MERCY

'If I were better, it would be better.' This is the soundtrack that plays in the background of many of our lives. There's an unconscious belief that everything that isn't good enough is so because *we're* not good enough. This results in a constant and self-imposed pressure to be better in an attempt to make everything and everyone in the world around us better too. Judging ourselves without mercy means we never give ourselves a break. No matter how well we do, it isn't well enough. No matter how much we achieve, it isn't enough. We're constantly trying to prove ourselves – mostly to ourselves.

This is one of the defining features of adult children and of people vulnerable to burnout. No matter how well other people think we do, we think we could do better. If we get mostly excellent results on a test or in a performance evaluation, we'll ignore all the good points and dwell on the ones we didn't do so well in.

A close companion of merciless judgement is perfectionism. We expect ourselves to do everything perfectly. And not only do we want things to be perfect, we also want them to be perfect immediately – there's no learning curve for us. There's also no sense that we can ask for help from people who are more experienced or who may know better.

This total and complete (and impossible) pressure to be perfect from the outset is paralysing, because when we set ourselves up to do something perfectly the first time, we set ourselves up for fear, insecurity and anxiety. We set ourselves up to stop before we've even started.

Judging ourselves without mercy means that we push ourselves beyond any and all sensible limits. It's never enough, and we can never take a well-earned and deserved break.

4. WE CONSTANTLY SEEK APPROVAL AND AFFIRMATION FROM OTHERS

We not only judge ourselves mercilessly, we also constantly seek approval and affirmation from others. This causes us to try harder and do more in order to get the attention we crave. We take on extra tasks at work. We take on extra family responsibilities. We assume more responsibility for the smooth running of our relationships.

In our quest to be noticed and appreciated by everyone around us, we push ourselves to the brink.

5. WE TAKE OURSELVES VERY SERIOUSLY AND HAVE A HARD TIME HAVING FUN

It's hard to know which comes first. Do we have a hard time having fun because we take ourselves so seriously? Or do we take ourselves so seriously because fun is so hard for us to have? Do we stay at work so long because we don't have enough leisure activities? Or do we not have enough leisure activities because we work such long hours? Whichever comes first, the result is that we often don't give ourselves enough downtime.

Let's look at the example of Sipho, whose job has, over the last few years, got more and more demanding. At about the same time that the job demands started to grow, Sipho went through a shattering breakup. He was so devastated by the end of his relationship that he threw himself into his work, taking on extra responsibilities, signing up for overtime and enrolling in training programme after training programme. Before he knew it, he was spending 16 hours a day working or in class, six days a week. And on the seventh day he was so tired after doing his laundry, shopping and general living-related administration that all he could do in the time left to him was rest. He had no energy or enthusiasm for seeing friends, playing sport or doing any of the things that used to bring him pleasure.

A year after the breakup, Sipho thought it would be nice to spend the couple of evenings a week that had opened up after he had completed one of his courses (with distinction, obviously) seeing friends, playing a game of squash and maybe going out to dinner and a concert every now and then. But in his absence his friends had found other things to do and other people to do them with, and Sipho found himself alone and lonely with time to fill. And fill it he did – by signing up for another class.

In this way, Sipho painted himself into a corner. He was exhausted, stressed and lonely. He desperately needed to take some time off work to rest and relax and to spend time doing things that fed his soul, with people who nurtured him and made him feel loved. But he was too scared by the empty space to take time off. He was too exhausted to keep working the way he'd been and was too vulnerable to go on holiday alone. He really was in a burnout pickle and couldn't see how to get himself out of it. It's hard to have fun when there is no time or space to have it in.

6. WE'RE INTENSELY LOYAL EVEN WHEN IT'S OBVIOUS THAT OUR LOYALTY IS MISPLACED

Because we're so loyal, we tend to stay in situations – jobs, relationships – far longer than we should. Even when it's obvious that the situation isn't good for us and may even be negatively affecting our physical and/or emotional health, we stay there in the hope that things will improve – and possibly in the belief that 'if I were better, it would be better'.

We make excuses for everything and everyone – except ourselves, of course. Our bosses aren't bullies, they're 'stressed'. Our friends aren't selfish, they're 'busy'. Our love interest isn't uninterested, s/he's 'scared'. If someone lets us down or disappoints us, it must be our fault.

Forcing ourselves to stay in a place that a larger and wiser part of ourselves is aching to leave uses up an enormous amount of energy, creates massive internal conflict, and ends up building resentment that's only ever unhelpful and toxic – all of which, over time, contribute to burnout.

7. WE CAN BE VERY IMPULSIVE AND OFTEN AGREE TO DOING SOMETHING WITHOUT GIVING IT ENOUGH THOUGHT

In our quest to help everyone, be agreeable, not disappoint, and pretend that we can do everything that others want us to, we often find ourselves agreeing to or signing up for things that we haven't thought through very well, and for which we certainly haven't given much thought about the consequences of.

And then, because we judge ourselves without mercy, don't like to admit we need help, are intensely loyal and aren't always very good at telling ourselves or anyone else the truth, we don't allow ourselves to change our minds or follow a different path. This means that we stay stuck in situations of our own making that may be making us anxious, angry or stressed – all of which, over time, also contribute to burnout.

8. WE'RE EITHER IRRESPONSIBLE OR INCREDIBLY RESPONSIBLE

Actually, we're usually both. We're generally incredibly responsible when it comes to considering the needs, wellbeing and demands of others, and incredibly irresponsible when it comes to taking care of ourselves. We're reliable and dependable, and work ourselves into the ground. We're caring and considerate of others, and uncaring and inconsiderate of ourselves. We take responsibility for the happiness of others and feel angry when no one does the same for us.

Adult children are generally very aware of, and responsive to, the needs of others – more often than not at our own expense. This tendency to what I call 'others-centredness' is an enormous contributor to exhaustion and burnout.

9. WE STRUGGLE WITH ASKING FOR HELP

More than two decades ago, when I was in my 20s, tiny (I weighed 45kg), and trying very hard to prove myself in a male environment, I spent two weeks on a study tour in Denmark with 14 policemen. Every morning I came down from my hotel room, struggling to carry my heavy and bulky suitcase. Every morning 14 big, strong men offered to assist. Every morning I turned down their offers to help me with my baggage (pun intended). Had I accepted, I would've avoided a lot of back pain, and been able to build stronger and more reciprocal relationships with my colleagues.

Adult children often prefer to be the helper rather than the one who's being helped. We find it easier to be helpful – sometimes we even feel the need to be indispensable so that we're not forgotten about – than to allow ourselves to be helped.

We struggle to ask for help because we think that the request might be ignored, rejected or scorned. Maybe we'll be seen as weak. Maybe we'll let down our guard and end up getting hurt.

Sometimes we just don't think at all. We're so used to looking after ourselves and everyone around us that it just doesn't occur to us to ask for help.

Sometimes – often – we actively turn down offers of assistance. We don't want to appear weak or needy or demanding or incapable. We need to keep up the pretence of being able to look after ourselves and everyone else, even when it's not true.

Sometimes we're so attached to our own struggles, and the unhelpful thoughts and behaviour patterns that perpetuate them, that we can't allow ourselves to put down that burden by asking for and accepting help that's available to us. We reject ourselves as well as the people trying to help us.

SOUND FAMILIAR?

Do any of these 9 characteristics ring true for you? If so, which ones may be contributing to your overwork, overwhelm and overcommitment?

'If I were better, it would be better'

While it may be true that many of our characteristics and habits make us prone to burnout, it's also true that we're very resourceful, creative and reliable problem-solvers. When we put our minds to getting something done, we do it. And that's why we're not only likely to develop burnout, we can also rely on ourselves to do whatever we need to do to recover and learn from it.

Which of the statements below ring true for you?
1. I never manage to do things right.
2. I feel that I can – and often do – ask for help.
3. I feel it's my fault when something goes wrong.
4. I have many people I can rely on to help me when I need it.
5. When someone disappoints me, I feel responsible.
6. I allow myself to do what I really want.
7. I need to make sure that everyone around me is happy and well looked after all the time.
8. I feel comfortable saying no to things that I don't want to do.
9. I have to do things myself if I want them done properly.
10. I feel comfortable and unapologetic about all the good things in my life.

If some of the even-numbered statements ring true for you, then you have good boundaries and a healthy approach to navigating your way through life. It shows that you're able to ask for (and accept) help, and that you can say no to things that aren't good for you or that you don't want to do. If all of the even-numbered statements ring true for you, you're probably not burned out and are not likely to become burned out if you're able to maintain these healthy thoughts and boundaries.

If the odd-numbered statements apply to you, however, it's a strong indication of the likelihood of burnout – happened, happening or on its way. These limiting beliefs are all important (and very common) reasons for us trying to do more, be more, achieve more. They're based on the larger, more foundational limiting belief of 'if I were better, it would be better' that underpins many of the others-centred choices and actions we take and make: 'If I were thinner, s/he'd love me more'; 'If I made more money, s/he'd be happier'; 'If I were smarter, I'd be more respected'; 'If I do everything perfectly then things will get better'.

'If I were better, it would be better' is the reason we feel we can't ask for help – because if we were better, then surely we wouldn't need help? It's the reason we feel we can't say no – because how can we be better if we say no to others?

Learning to say no, and asking for help

I believe that not asking for help and not saying no are two of the largest contributors to burnout. This is true in all areas of our lives – home, work, friends, community. When we feel we have to do everything ourselves, we don't share the load. When we feel we can't say no to anything, it adds to our already overlarge burden.

One reason we feel we can't ask for help is a fear that we may be seen as weak or not good enough. Another is that we want to protect others from having to do whatever it is that we need help with. And yet another is that we may feel that there's no one we can rely on to provide us with the help we need. So we do it all ourselves, partly to protect ourselves and partly to protect others.

ASKING FOR HELP TO ASK FOR HELP

If you're a person who struggles to say no or ask for help, have this conversation with yourself.

'I know that I struggle to ask for help, especially when I need it most. I know that I tend to say yes to requests from people I love before I even think about whether or not I want to do whatever it is they're asking of me.

'Not asking for help and not allowing myself to consider if I would rather say no than yes can make me overcommitted to things that I don't enjoy doing and which aren't good for me to do (they're the *wrong things*), which contributes to my exhaustion and feeling of being overwhelmed.

'I'm going to speak to the most important people in my life and the people I trust the most. I'll explain that I struggle to ask for help, especially when I'm most in need of it, and that I struggle to say no. I'll suggest that when they can see I need help, they offer it in a way that helps me to accept it. If they ask me to do something, it would be useful if they could explain how important it is to them, so I can assess whether to say yes or no.

'I'm going to ask them for help in asking for help and saying no.'

Are your feelings really yours?

I was in my 40s when I realised that not all of the emotional and physical discomfort I experienced belonged to me all the time. Often a client would walk into my office and, seemingly out of the blue, I'd start to feel an overwhelming sense of exhaustion. From being full of energy and vitality, I'd struggle to keep my eyes open. When I asked if the client was feeling tired (a relatively safe bet, given the number of clients I see with burnout), the answer was always yes.

Once, I visited a friend in hospital who'd just given birth. From being happy and excited about a brand-new being, suddenly I felt hopeless and desperate. Feeling slightly panicked, I looked around the hospital room, and when I caught sight of the new mom in the next bed, I whispered to my friend, 'Does your neighbour have postnatal depression?' She answered, 'Yes – the doctors have been really worried about her.'

After a lifetime of unexplained and inexplicable anxiety, insomnia, exhaustion and various physical symptoms, the penny finally dropped: I feel what the people around me feel.

People, particularly adult children, who are vulnerable to burnout are often what psychiatrist Judith Orloff refers to as 'intuitive empaths' – people who feel what other people are feeling. Without needing to be told, and often without even being aware of it, intuitive empaths often experience the emotions, anxieties and physical sensations that the people they're with are going through.

Being an intuitive empath is a gift – it helps you to be truly empathic and understanding of what everyone in your life is going through. But it can also be a curse – you may be a sponge for all the feelings you're exposed to, particularly the negative ones. And that, as you can imagine – or maybe you know this for yourself – is very, very tiring and draining.

Negative or challenging emotions are hard enough to bear when they belong to us, but when we pick up and carry the difficult feelings of everyone around us as well, we're embarking on a rapid journey to exhaustion and burnout.

Being responsible only for your own feelings and emotions is very liberating. You'll see an immediate improvement in your mood and your energy levels when you've mastered the art of putting down or returning feelings that don't belong to you.

WHAT ARE YOU FEELING?

Next time you feel a sensation or an emotion that seems inappropriate for you at that time, sit quietly, tune in to your body and do the following.

1. Name what you're feeling.
2. Get clear on if the feeling is emotional (happy, sad, angry, anxious) or physical (hungry, tired, headachy, hot).
3. Ask yourself, 'Does this feeling belong to me?' If the answer is yes, you can decide how to address the feeling. If the answer is no, put the feeling down – literally imagine yourself bending down and placing the feeling on the floor and walking away from it. It may help to wash your hands of it by literally washing your hands.

Here's an example:
1. I'm feeling tired. Also hungry. Also sad.
2. The tiredness and hunger are physical. The sadness is emotional.
3. The tiredness and hunger belong to me because I haven't eaten yet today – having a good breakfast will address them both. The sadness isn't mine; it belongs to a good friend who's grieving the shocking death of a relative – I'm going to send her a message telling her I'm thinking of her, then I can put down the feeling and walk away from it. Excuse me while I go and wash my hands and then have something to eat.

COME TO YOUR SENSES

When you 'come to your senses', you return to your body and feel more grounded. A quick and easy way to do this is a 'sense drench'.

Right now, as you sit where you're sitting, bring to mind and, as far as possible, try to experience the sensations of your favourite:

* Smells
* Tastes
* Sounds
* Textures
* Sights

Now try to create a felt experience in your mind that combines all of them, for example, 'I'm going for a walk in my lunch hour. I'm taking in the deep blue sky, the way everything looks clear and just-washed after a soaking Joburg thunderstorm; the colours seem brighter and everything looks shiny. I can feel the soft air on my skin. If I listen very hard, I can hear birdsong among the insistent beeping of the taxi drivers demanding attention from potential passengers. I can smell the scent of the jasmine that's currently in bloom. I feel pleasantly hungry and I'm looking forward to my lunch.'

Try to do this every time you're feeling stressed, stretched or sad. And even if you aren't feeling any challenging emotions, try to come to your senses at least once or twice a day.

2

The road to burnout is paved with good intentions

As a child growing up in a very poor, underserviced and often chaotic township in South Africa, Kati had had visions of doing the kind of work that ensured that poor and disadvantaged people received legal representation that they would otherwise not be able to afford. After she became a lawyer, though, she found herself in the midst of a highly contested commercial litigation that went on for more than a year. For Kati, what started off as tiredness and stress escalated into extreme exhaustion.

Normally a calm, measured and cheerful person, over the course of the year, she became irritable, panicky, picky and pessimistic. She stopped seeing her friends. She stopped going to the gym before work. She stopped ensuring there was healthy food for her and her family to eat. She stopped going to book club. She stopped reading. She stopped laughing. She stopped everything that used to bring her, and the people around her, pleasure.

Kati started consuming way too much sugar, carbs and caffeine. She put on weight around her middle. She felt moody and depressed. She picked fights with her nearest and dearest. She became so irritable and irrational that even the dog avoided being in the same room as her. She stayed at home every night, falling asleep in front of the TV, and struggled to get out of bed in the mornings.

From being a passionate person who was totally committed to and enthusiastic about every aspect of her life, Kati became someone who couldn't see the point of very much. Everything felt heavy and oppressive and like too much effort.

Kati had burnout, and it affected her in every realm of her life – physical, mental, emotional, spiritual and relational. And, as most burnout sufferers do, instead of asking for help or slowing down when she started to feel overwhelmed, Kati pushed herself even harder. She tried harder, fought harder, worked longer hours.

One day she just couldn't get out of bed. She couldn't summon up the energy to phone her boss and say she was taking a sick day. She couldn't stop crying. She couldn't do anything but sleep or stare out the window.

Kati was lucky – she was able to recognise that it wasn't only her body and mind that were tired, it was also her soul and spirit that felt eroded by doing work that didn't feel meaningful. She didn't, as so many burnout deniers do, develop diabetes, suffer a stroke or heart attack, become clinically depressed or go through a divorce. She was able to take time off and restore her body, mind and soul to relative health. She had the means and the social and financial wherewithal to stop everything (and I really do mean *everything*) and spend eight weeks resting, sleeping and nourishing herself.

It took two months of doing absolutely nothing every single day – two months of being almost entirely confined to her bed or the couch – before Kati started to feel like herself again. She was able to recover her energy and enthusiasm. Her next challenge, that of maintaining it, will be a lifelong one.

Burnout isn't like chickenpox: you don't just wake up with it one morning. It takes a long time to develop – and, unfortunately, it takes a long time to recover from. And even when you've recovered and are feeling better, you'll always be prone to redeveloping burnout. This is partly because once you've experienced burnout, you develop a kind of burnout-induced frailty, but it's largely because of who you are and how you are in the world. It was your thoughts, behaviours and beliefs that caused round one of burnout, and without understanding and changing those, you'll be destined to revisit and re-experience the horrors of the condition – maybe even over and over again.

Since the 1970s, when the term 'burnout' was first coined by psychologist Herbert Freudenberger, our understanding of the condition has evolved. Early on, it was used largely in relation to people working in the caring professions – doctors, social workers, psychologists, caregivers. Freudenberger noticed that people who worked with other people's pain and discomfort were easily burned out themselves as a result of exposure to other people's worries and woes. The concept spread rapidly and soon came to also be associated with businesspeople who were overworked, stressed and exhausted.

Today, burnout is used to describe the overwhelming physical, emotional and mental feelings that affect people who work in any and all kinds of high-stress environments. I describe burnout as feeling tired from life, because it's our lives and how we live them that cause us to become burned out.

I don't believe that burnout affects only people who're suffering from career fatigue. Burnout is an equal-opportunity condition and doesn't discriminate in whom it chooses. I've coached burnout sufferers who are high-flying executives, retired folk, university students, entrepreneurs, fulltime stay-at-home moms, and people who are out of work. Those affected by burnout are as diverse as any population. What they have in common, however, is *an inability to prioritise their own needs and desires.*

The 5 whys

One of my favourite movies is *Groundhog Day*, in which the character played by Bill Murray keeps waking up on the same day, in the same place, doing the same thing, meeting the same girl and making the same mistakes, over and over again. He only manages to escape this circle of sameness when he works out what it is that he needs to change at a fundamental level.

I often see clients who, just like Bill Murray's character in the movie, have been coming up against the same barriers in their lives, no matter how many ways they've tried to get around them. They've felt bored or unsatisfied by all of their many and varied jobs. They've felt misunderstood and underappreciated in all of their many and varied relationships. They've felt unhealthy and unattractive despite all of their many and varied eating plans.

If you don't understand what's causing the problem in the first place, you won't be able to make it go away. Unless you understand what the barriers are, and why they're there, they're going to keep appearing – day after day, month after month, and even year after year. Trust me when I say that at least nine-tenths of the battle is won when you've worked out what the problem is.

The secret is in the 'why?'

Pick a problem – any problem – and ask 'why?' a few times, and you'll get to the bottom of it. For example, ask yourself why you're tired.

Why am I tired? Because I didn't get enough sleep last night.

Why didn't I get enough sleep last night? Because I have insomnia.

Why do I have insomnia? Because I can't calm my mind down enough to go to sleep.

Why is my mind so busy? Because I was working on a writing project until 10pm and then I was too wired to sleep.

Why was I working so late? Because I'd procrastinated, and was in danger of missing my deadline on the project.

By the fifth 'why?' you should have a real sense of the underlying problem – and what the solutions could be. In this example, you may need to schedule your time better.

Acknowledge your spirit

One of the most important steps in recovering from burnout is to reconnect with yourself and your spirit.

It's difficult to define 'spirit' – is it your soul, your personality, your character, your intellect? I think that, quite simply, your spirit is the part of you that makes you you. It's the part of you that picks you up when you feel down, that helps you judge right from wrong, that finds meaning in your world and relationships. It's made up of many immeasurable aspects of you: your values, your beliefs, your interests, your fears, your aspirations, your desires … it's your essence.

In all the excitement and stress of our demanding lives, it's easy to forget about this aspect of ourselves. The emotional, mental, physical and relational realms often speak louder and are more demanding, so they take precedence in our lives. There's often so much noise in our external world that we forget to pay attention to our internal world. I firmly believe that burnout is a result of becoming disconnected from ourselves. When we're disconnected and dis-integrated, our boundaries become weak and easy to violate.

WRITE TO RECONNECT WITH YOURSELF

I've long been a fan of *The Artist's Way* author Julia Cameron. Her 'morning pages' are my most often prescribed homework for my coaching clients. The idea is to write three pages — with a pen and on actual paper — every morning on first waking up.

Because the aim of the writing is to reconnect with our inner voice, what you write isn't nearly as important as the act of writing. Something very magical happens when we put pen to paper: after a while (sometimes minutes, sometimes days or weeks) it feels as though our pen has taken on a life of its own. We become a witness to what's appearing on the page, rather than the driver.

Ideally, you should write before you've properly woken up, when your subconscious is still strong and has a voice. But writing at any time is always useful and powerful.

A little bit of nothing goes a long way

I'm an enormous fan of a daily practice of quiet time. It changed my life and I know that it will change yours, too. It can be prayer, meditation, journalling, a gentle walk, sitting outside with a cup of tea or coffee before you start your day... Even if you can only spare 10 minutes, anything that allows you to be alone and turn inwards is a very good way of reconnecting with your spirit and remembering what matters to you.

Take the example of Jackie, who was experiencing that sense of helplessness and hopelessness that comes with feeling out of control. No matter how hard she tried to impose order on her life, it just wasn't working. It's a common mistake that many of us make. When we feel anxious and out of control, we try to bring back a sense of order by *doing* more, when what we really need is to just *be* more.

Jackie had spent many years sprinting away from her feelings. She'd been running so far, so fast and so frequently that when I asked her to spend 20 minutes every day doing nothing, her face told a story of sheer panic. She literally started to hyperventilate and looked as though she may burst into tears just at the thought of being alone with her thoughts and emotions. The idea of 20 minutes of unfilled and 'unproductive' time was too scary, so I suggested that she try turning off the radio in her car and driving in silence (no phone calls either) for part of her morning or evening commute. I also suggested that she start with 5 minutes and work her way up to 20.

Slowly but surely, Jackie was able to work her way up to 20 silent minutes in the car, after which she was able to spend 20 silent minutes with herself every morning. Between waking and showering, she was able to go outside and sit and check in with herself while drinking her morning coffee and listening to the birds. After just one week of spending time alone in peace and quiet, Jackie found that she was feeling calmer and more centred. She was able to respond to all her many and varied demands in a more mindful and effective way. She was less anxious and more able to weather various emotional storms with an elegance and grace she'd forgotten she had.

She now does this every day, as she recognises that those 20 minutes are essential in helping her to connect with herself – her body, her mind and her spirit – and to establish exactly what she needs to give herself every day in order to maintain her happiness and health.

We all know that feeling of being overwhelmed: of having so much to do that we don't know where to start, of having so many people to look after that we aren't able to think about, let alone look after, ourselves and our own needs.

We all get that feeling from time to time. Our instinct when we have too much to do and not enough time to do it in is usually to try harder to be more effective and get more things done. We get up earlier. We work harder. We write more lists.

But we can't make the best choices when we're in a panic-driven, exhaustion-fuelled state of mind and body. All that happens when we keep pushing ourselves harder and further is that eventually we become so tired and stressed and freaked out that we hit the burnout wall and have to stop. And it's only then that we allow ourselves to rest and regroup, and to start making healthy choices that allow us to be more efficient and effective. Sadly, it's often only when we've broken our spirits, sometimes thoroughly and completely, that we allow ourselves to build them up again.

The good news is, no matter how removed you may feel from yourself and your spirit, it's relatively easy to reconnect. Your spirit never leaves you, even if it sometimes may feel as though it's gone AWOL. All you need to do is get still and quiet to remember who you really are and what's important to you.

It can be very hard and uncomfortable for some people to be alone with themselves at first. We're so out of practice that it may even feel a little scary. If this is the case with you, it may help to go for a gentle walk – by yourself and in silence. Or you could do what Jackie did and start by turning off all sound in the car as you drive to or from work. You could sit down with a journal and pen and write about what comes up for you. Or you could have a candle-lit bath. It doesn't matter how you create the island of nothing, as long as you create it regularly – because when you've done enough of nothing, you'll be able to do everything that much better.

HOW TO DO NOTHING

By doing nothing, you create the space to tune into your body and hear what it's asking you to do for it.

Go somewhere quiet where you can be alone with yourself. Turn off the radio, the TV, your computer. Put your phone in a place where you can't see or hear it.

Don't talk to anyone but yourself.

Don't listen to anyone but yourself.

Don't go anywhere but inside yourself.

Was it hard? Was it easy? When and where did you find the time? What happened to you when you got still and quiet? What insights and messages did you hear?

NURTURE YOURSELF WITH NATURE

When clients come to me suffering from exhaustion, burnout, and feelings of disconnection or being stuck, the first thing I recommend is that they spend time every day in nature. They don't have to do anything there (in fact, the less they do, the better), they just have to *be* there. Because there's nothing that brings us back to ourselves and calms us down more than being outside and in the elements.

Diarist Anne Frank wrote:

> 'The best remedy for those who are afraid, lonely or unhappy is to go outside, somewhere where they can be quite alone with the heavens, nature and God. Because only then does one feel that all is as it should be and that God wishes to see people happy, amidst the simple beauty of nature. As long as this exists, and it certainly always will, I know that then there will always be comfort for every sorrow, whatever the circumstances may be. And I firmly believe that nature brings solace in all troubles.'

Think less, feel more

All too often, we allow our bodies to be hijacked by our minds.

Mental agility is very useful and serves us well for the most part. It helps us to get the job done, even when we don't feel like doing it. It allows us to forgive those we love, even when we feel mortally wounded by them. It allows us to push through the physical discomfort and finish running that marathon. But it also encourages us to ignore a very real, very honest source of information and feedback about our lives and how we choose to live them. We can – and do – talk ourselves into or out of anything. We can convince ourselves to do things that don't feel right for us, and we can convince ourselves to not do things that do feel right for us.

Have you ever just known that something you were doing or thinking about doing was a bad idea? Did you have a bad feeling in the pit of your stomach? Was your heart pounding, your blood roaring in your ears? Did you start feeling weak and shaky? Did you break out in a sweat?

And did you go ahead and do it anyway?

Most of us have. Not just once, but many times. Over and over again, my clients tell me about occasions when they ignored what their bodies were telling them and pursued a path that ended in misery and stress.

In retrospect, we can see that there were clear 'do not enter' signs at the entrance to some of the roads we chose to take, but we talked ourselves into going down those roads and doing things that we didn't want to do. We told ourselves that we should do it because that's what grownups do. It's what everyone expects of us. If we didn't do it, we'd be hurting someone's feelings.

By the same token, we also talk ourselves out of the things that we do want to do. We shouldn't do it because it isn't what grownups do. Everyone expects us to be doing something else. We don't want to hurt anyone's feelings...

Our bodies reinforce the messages our inner voice wants us to hear. When we're able to make the space to reconnect with ourselves, we allow ourselves to connect with our bodies and listen to what they want us to know. None of us would experience burnout if we paid attention, and responded respectfully, to how our bodies feel. If we stopped pushing ourselves when we were weak, if we said no to things that were bad for us, if we ate when we were hungry, drank when we were thirsty and went to bed when we were tired, we wouldn't reach the point of having nothing left to give.

Instead, we tell ourselves we need to finish one last thing before leaving work. We convince ourselves that we can stay awake through the late movie. We drug ourselves with caffeine, sugar and carbohydrates to give our bodies more fuel to carry on, even when we're beyond the point of exhaustion. We ignore the signals that our bodies send us, from 'I'm tired and need a rest' (we just keep pushing ourselves to carry on, abusing sugar and caffeine to help us on our way) to 'I hate doing this job so much that it's making me sick' (we remind ourselves that the job we hate doing is what pays the bills).

We ignore, override and blatantly disregard the messages our bodies send us, despite the fact that our bodies are a much more reliable source of information than our minds. Our minds can (and often do) tell us terrible fibs, but our bodies never lie.

Thandi was one of my more anxious clients. She was passionate about her work as a primary-school teacher, even though she found it very intense at times. She was clever, precise and slender to the point of being unhealthy. She also suffered from frequent colds and migraines. At first I thought that her thinness was intentional; it seemed to me that nobody could be that skinny without a lot of effort. But I gradually came to realise that, although intention had a hand in the problem, it wasn't how I imagined.

Thandi came rushing in to her late-evening session one day, flustered and all over the place. I asked her to sit quietly for a moment and then, when she'd come back to herself, I asked her to tell me what she was feeling in her body. She struggled to connect with her physical sensations at first, instead telling me she was stressed, busy and overworked. After a while she was able to re-enter her body, and she recognised that she was hungry, thirsty and had a headache (which, we worked out, was a result of being dehydrated). Nothing had passed her lips since a very rushed breakfast of coffee and a muffin 12 hours earlier.

Thandi was intent on being the very best teacher and role model she could be. She filled every minute of the day with planning lessons, setting tests, marking tests, her pupils, her colleagues, school extramurals and parent meetings. She made no time to eat or drink; even during breaks she was busy helping children with extra lessons or listening to their troubles and worries. It was no wonder she was so thin.

When Thandi learned to tune in to her body and respond to what it was saying to her, she was able to drastically reduce the frequency of her migraines and colds – just by giving her body what it needed. And while she remained slim, she was able to turn back the tide of the burnout that had been creeping up on her. If she hadn't been able to do this, her burnout would've progressed, and she may well have mistaken the discomfort of not looking after herself properly for some sort of dissatisfaction with her job – and the education system may have lost a talented and dedicated teacher for no good reason.

We can't get better and burnout-free if we don't respect our physical bodies. Many of the burnout clients I work with are so disconnected from their bodies that they can't even tell me if they're warm or cool enough, let alone tune in to subtler messages their bodies are sending them. Often, it's only when I ask them to consciously connect with their body and feel what it's feeling, that they realise that they're hungry or tired or headachy or sad – and have been for quite some time.

LISTEN TO YOUR BODY

Most of us need to re-learn to listen to our bodies. And once we've heard what our bodies are telling us, we need to believe, trust and respond appropriately. We need to rest when we're tired, eat and drink (healthily) when we're hungry and thirsty, support ourselves when we're in pain.

Identifying how we're feeling and understanding why we're feeling that way empowers us to take action to address the feeling. Every day, at least once a day, get quiet and still and pay attention to your body.

Ask yourself:
1. What am I feeling? (Am I experiencing any pain or discomfort? If so, where, and what exactly does it feel like? Am I hot/cold/tired/hungry/thirsty?)
2. Why do I feel this way? (Did I overtrain at gym yesterday? Did I sleep badly last night? Do I have tense shoulders because I'm angry with a friend or family member?)
3. What do I want to do about it? (Do I need a rest day, or to have a nap this afternoon, or should I say no to seeing that friend this week?)

Prevention is better than cure

If you feel you're on the road to burnout, there's a lot that you can do to stop going any farther down that path. And if you intervene soon enough, you should be able to reverse any burnout symptoms you may already be experiencing.

The most powerful and effective intervention tool for burnout recovery and prevention is awareness. When you raise your awareness about your own needs and wants, and are able to pause and think about the demands that are being placed on you, you'll be able to respond thoughtfully, rather than reacting impulsively, in a manner that's supportive of you.

Kati loved her career, was extremely good at what she did and felt she could make a positive contribution to her country and the world. But precisely because of this passion and prowess, she was promoted into a position that bore little resemblance to the job she'd originally signed up for. Before she knew it, she found herself in courtrooms with people she didn't like or respect, being expected to argue for things that she didn't believe in. So it wasn't just the long hours and the stressful environment that diminished her life force, it was also the erosion of her principles, her values and even her character.

I'm convinced that burnout is a matter of boundaries and integrity. We get burnout as a consequence of not having firm enough boundaries. When we're not able to draw and maintain healthy and strong boundaries in our lives, we become vulnerable to burnout. When we're not able to protect, enact and honour our personal values and ethics, we become vulnerable to burnout. We need to work out our own limitations and capacity, and work with them rather than against them. We have to get clear on what we can and can't manage, and set up the systems we need to do and be our best.

All of the obvious causes of burnout that you can read about almost anywhere include stress, being overwhelmed, physical and mental exhaustion, poor diet, poor sleeping habits, poor work/life balance, lack of control, stressful relationships, lack of social support, mismatch in values, doing a job you hate or don't feel equipped to perform adequately, and feeling out of your depth.

All of these are integrity and boundary issues; they arise because of an inability to draw a clear boundary, an inability to know when to say no, an inability to ask for help, and an inability to make new choices.

In my observations and experience, burnout affects anybody who tries to do too much and, more importantly, tries to do too much of the wrong thing. When you consistently, and over time, persuade yourself into doing things that aren't good for you, and that don't make you happy, or talk yourself out of doing those things that *are* good for you and *do* make you happy, you open yourself up to burnout.

THE NEED FOR NO

When you do the wrong things (and by this I mean the things that are wrong for you), be it at home, at work, in love or in the world, you create an ongoing tension between what you want to do and what you tell yourself to do. And it's exhausting.

Author and motivator Byron Katie says, 'Saying "no" to someone else is saying "yes" to you.' This aptly captures the tension we create when we say yes to others at our own expense. Put differently, a yes to someone else is often a no to yourself.

So very often, I hear clients talk about how they find themselves doing jobs they hate, or being in relationships that make them miserable, or climbing a mountain that terrifies them. Even staying up late to keep a partner company instead of going to bed when we're tired is a way of saying yes to someone else at our own expense. We frequently say yes when we want to say no because we think (often quite erroneously) that it will make someone else happy. I'm all for helping other people to be happy, with one proviso: it can't be at our own expense.

Why do we find it so hard to say no to others? I believe it's for a number of reasons. We feel bad about letting other people down. We worry that if we say no we may never be asked again. We worry that the person we say no to may be cross with us or punish us in some way. We think we need to have a good reason for not doing something we're invited to do…

Feeling like we need a good reason or excuse for turning down an offer or invitation is what often gets us into trouble. 'I'd so love to come to the baby shower for your fourth child, but I have to fetch my great-aunt from the airport,' we may explain. To which the mother of the soon-to-be-born baby might respond, 'Well, bring her along to the party!' And then you have to invent another excuse. (What was that about lying when it would be just as easy to tell the truth?)

The truth is that you really don't have to explain yourself to anyone. All you need to say is 'Thank you for the invitation; I'm sorry I won't be able to make it' or 'Thanks so much for the invitation; I already have plans so I won't be able to join you'. You may know that you aren't able to make it because you're planning a couple of hours on the couch with a book; you don't have to tell them that. *Why* you say no is none of their business.

Perhaps more damaging is saying no when we want to say yes. An example of this is turning down an invitation to spend time on the weekend or in the evenings with family and friends because of too much work. Another is passing up an opportunity to do something so that someone else gets that chance. Then there's depriving ourselves of comfort and enjoyment to try to make up for all the unhappiness and lack we see around us. These are some of the many, many ways we say no to ourselves when we really want to say yes.

SAY YES TO YOU

Practise saying no to things that don't serve you, and yes to things that do. Every day, choose at least one thing to which you give yourself permission to say no. It can be tiny or substantial — the choice is up to you.

You could say no to:
* Answering a call from a friend who you know drains you.
* Staying up late to watch a favourite late-night programme — rather record it so that you can go to bed at a reasonable hour.
* Staying at work to finish that last thing — leave at going-home time instead.
* Taking work home with you — spend time with people you love instead.
* An invitation to a social event you don't want to attend — rather spend the time doing something you love.
* Fast food — feed yourself something nourishing instead.
* Staying in a job you don't like — brush up that CV.

Some years ago, I found myself feeling disappointed and pretty much useless on every level. Everything felt like a mess, and physically, mentally and emotionally I'd run out of steam.

I'd been working with South African police officers for more than a decade and not only was I experiencing my own exhaustion, stress and frustration, I was also (being an empath) feeling the stress and trauma of all the law-enforcement men and women I'd come into contact with. And South African police officers are a very stressed and traumatised bunch.

I thought I was depressed. Terrified by how worthless and meaningless I felt, I went to my doctor to ask him for any kind of medicine that would make me feel less desperate and miserable. Being the wise and gifted healer that he is, he refused my request for a prescription and told me, 'You aren't depressed. You're having a spiritual crisis. You need to take some time off and decide what you want to do with your life.'

I left his rooms empty-handed, and in equal parts irritated (who doesn't want a quick fix when we feel so awful?) and relieved – because he was absolutely right: I *was* having a spiritual crisis. I was tired *from* my life, rather than *of* my life. I'd become so removed from myself and what belonged to me and what didn't, what I wanted and what was good for me, that my spirit was completely broken. And, as a consequence, I was suffering from total and utter burnout.

I dutifully took some time off and did nothing for a few weeks. I was so depleted that I couldn't even read (I usually read two or three books a week). I couldn't socialise. I couldn't exercise. All I could do was sleep and lie on my back looking at the sky. I wish this is an exaggeration, but it isn't. My burnout was all-embracing.

The only action I was able to take was writing my morning pages every day. Those 20 minutes of rambling onto a page were what kept me from falling apart completely. Every day, I felt a little more contained and a little less dis-integrated. And one day, miracle of miracles, while diligently capturing my stream of consciousness in my journal, my pen and my hand reminded me that I'd wanted to become a life coach for what felt like forever. Ever since I'd discovered life coach

Martha Beck, I knew that I was supposed to do that work, but I'd hidden that knowledge from myself while I threw myself into being the very best candidate for burnout I could be. A combination of my extreme loyalty, and my deeply held belief in and commitment to contributing to the still relatively young democratic South Africa, had kept me in an environment way past my sell-by date.

Now, thanks to my doctor and the space he'd encouraged me to create for myself, I was able to remember what was important to and for me – and to recognise that there were and are many other ways to honour my commitment to contributing while also honouring myself.

Wondrously, I was reintegrating. I was reunited with myself and my spirit was on the mend.

WHO ARE YOU?

When was the last time you thought about yourself — what makes you happy, what drives you, what feels meaningful to you in your life?

In the humdrum, stress and pressure of everyday life we can become so focused on external demands and other people's priorities that we forget about ourselves and our own needs and wants. Spend a couple of minutes reminding yourself who you are.

Ask yourself:
1. What's your favourite colour?
2. What song makes you sing along joyfully when you hear it on the radio?
3. If you could have one magical power, what would it be?
4. If you could invite any six people, living or dead, to a dinner party, who would you ask?
5. What would you serve them to eat and drink?

Answering these simple and seemingly silly questions will help you to reconnect with yourself and remember what you like and what's important to you.

SIT LESS, MOVE MORE

How long did you sit for today, working, worrying, thinking, stressing? Or maybe surfing the net, endlessly refreshing your Twitter or Facebook feed, earning your PhD in procrastination? Or in meetings, on phone calls or in your car?

No matter how active your brain is, if you aren't moving your body, you aren't looking after yourself properly. Being sedentary slows down your metabolism, increasing your risk of weight gain; and the reduced oxygen in your bloodstream caused by just sitting still makes you bored and tired.

Even gentle exercise lets oxygen in and stress out, releases adrenaline and gets the blood flowing. It helps you sleep better and improves your appetite for healthy food. If you sit less and move more, you'll feel happier and more stimulated and will be more productive.

Aim to move for at least five minutes every hour.

There are many ways to move more:

* Walk to fetch your sandwich rather than asking for it to be delivered.
* Get up and walk to the window every 60 or 90 minutes.
* Have stand-up meetings where nobody sits down (they'll be over much quicker).
* Go to your colleague's office to talk to him or her rather than sending an email or WhatsApp.
* Meet a friend for a walk at lunch time.

3

Take back yourself

Many of us get burnout because we're wasting a great deal of energy on completing tasks that hold no meaning or importance for us. They don't feed us; instead, they put us into energy overdraft.

When I'm coaching, an hour feels like a moment and I feel physically stronger with every client I see (although sometimes I feel a little mentally and emotionally weary). When I'm doing my tax return, however, the minutes crawl past like hours, and I get a headache and sore shoulders, and end up in a bad mood.

When we do what we love and are good at, it feels good. When we do what we don't like and aren't good at, it feels bad. Unfortunately, many of us spend much of our time doing what we don't like. We have jobs that need to be done to pay the bills. We have relatives who need to be phoned to keep the peace. We have Brussels sprouts to eat to stay healthy. We all make compromises all the time.

I'm all for compromise – it's a vital part of any healthy relationship – *as long as it's not at your own expense*. I believe that over-compromising is one of the major reasons that so many of us are fed up, worn down and burned out. I keep repeating it because I believe it so strongly: burnout affects not only those of us who do too much, but more importantly, those of us who do *too much of the wrong things*.

Just like Kati, when you consistently, and over time, persuade yourself into doing things that aren't good for you, and that don't make you happy, or persuade yourself out of doing those things that *are* good for you and *do* make you happy, you open yourself up to burnout.

If you find yourself lacking energy and enthusiasm, it may be that you're tired from doing the right things for others and the wrong things for yourself. Getting over exhaustion requires, among other things, learning to listen to and honour yourself in order to do more of what feels good and less of what feels bad.

Track your energy

Identify the people, places and things that make you feel happy and energised, and those that make you feel unhappy, drained and overwhelmed.

Every time you're with someone, or even thinking about being with someone, feel how your body feels. Is it excited and full of energy, strong and powerful? Or is it heavy and tired and drained?

Pay attention, too, to how your body responds to all the places you go. Does the shopping mall make you feel full of beans or full of dread? Does going to a friend's house make you feel warm and fuzzy or itchy and scratchy?

And listen to what your body is telling you about tasks and activities. Pay attention to your energy levels throughout the day. From washing dishes to chairing a meeting, what's your body telling you about how much or how little you like doing that task?

Use the information your body is sharing with you to make good decisions about how and where you use your energy, so you can do less of what starves you and more of what feeds you. To do this, divide a page into three columns. Using a typical week as your reference point, identify all the people, places and activities you generally and routinely engage with. Once you've listed them all in the relevant columns, think about engaging with each of them and listen to what your body is telling you about them. What makes you feel good and what makes you feel bad (or even not so good)? Which of these people, places and activities feed you, and which starve you?

Here's an example from my own life.

People	Places	Activities
Uriah Heep (☹)	Shopping centre (☹)	Coaching (☺)
Jane Eyre (☺)	Garden (☺)	Tax returns (☹)
Anne Shirley (☺)	My consulting room (☺)	Watching MasterChef (☺)

You can use this knowledge to say no to the things that drain you and yes to those that feed you.

Deciding if and how to engage

The things that drain our energy aren't always big things; there are also lots of smaller things that we assume we must do or keep doing. When we interrogate our to-do lists, we're able to see many items that we could say no to or ask for help with: going clubbing, going to family events, attending every meeting we're invited to, answering every phone call (even when we're in the middle of something), acceding to all requests for a sympathetic ear by a draining or demanding friend, grocery shopping, ironing, mowing the lawn, finishing a book we hate.

Take another look at the last exercise. When it comes to energy-draining people, places and activities, first you have to decide *if* you want to engage with them at all; and of those you decide to keep on your to-do list, it is useful to think about *how* you want to engage with them in a way that's more supportive of your own needs and abilities.

So, for example, I'm going to try to stay away from Uriah Heep; and if I do have to see him, I'll make sure that I take someone with me and that I have a very good reason for leaving after 30 minutes. I'm going to give myself permission to not go to shopping centres any more – I'll shop in smaller places or online. And I'm not going to leave doing my tax return until the last minute; instead, I'm going to break it down into small and manageable chunks of time – 45 minutes every day for four days should be more than enough time.

When we say no to things that aren't important and/or drain our energy and make us unhappy, and ask for help (including from ourselves) in order to improve our quality of life, our lives improve dramatically. And when we start being more discerning about what we sign ourselves up for before we sign up, our lives improve even more dramatically.

STAY AWAY FROM HORROR-MONGERS

There are some people who thrive on drama and actively add to your anxiety by escalating any and every bit of bad news or gossip. Often dressing up their voyeuristic excitement as outrage, they dwell on the bad and brush over the good. They get off on making themselves and everyone around them feel worse.

Every office and workplace has at least one horror-monger. They will seek you out to fill you in on the latest rumour and scandal, corner you to invite you into their den of disaster, and drain every drop of optimism and enthusiasm from you.

Spending time with them will only make you feel anxious, stressed, despondent and desperate. Stay away from them!

Mark is in his late 40s. Like many of us at that age, he has a lot going on. He's a very dedicated husband to his wife, who has an equally busy career. He's dad to two boys, both now at university. He happily visits his parents – who live a two-hour drive away – every weekend. He has a big job and was recently promoted to an even bigger role. He plays social soccer every week.

When he came to see me, Mark also coached kids' soccer, sat on an induction committee at work, was enrolled in an art-appreciation course he rarely made it to, and was trying to give up smoking. And he really, really loved to run – he was trying to squeeze in a run every day but often he didn't have time to make it a long enough run and some days he wasn't able to find the time to run at all. He desperately wanted to run the 90km Comrades Ultramarathon but just couldn't find the time to train properly for it.

Mark came to me for coaching not because he had burnout, but because he knew that if he carried on the way he was, he'd have it very soon. He knew he was overstretched and in danger of reaching breaking point.

We quickly identified that he was overcommitted. And he wasn't just doing too much, he was also doing too many wrong-for-him things. We took some time to help him see where he was losing energy and where he was gaining it, and we identified three activities that were draining his battery: the induction committee, the soccer coaching and the art-appreciation course.

He explained (to himself as much as to me) that he'd been on the committee for 10 years, and not only was he no longer the most appropriate person for it, he also didn't have as much time for it now as he'd had in the past. When it came to the soccer coaching, it was something he'd been doing since his sons were little, when it had been a way to spend time with them and teach them the game he loved. As for the art-appreciation course – he'd signed up for it in a fit of enthusiasm after attending an exhibition that he'd felt particularly moved by but the lectures were at an inconvenient time and he struggled to make them, and he felt bad about that.

Being intensely loyal and having a tendency to judge himself without mercy (particularly when he felt he may not follow through with something that he'd started), Mark hadn't even considered changing his mind about any of these three commitments. I encouraged him to think about what he may safely be able to say no to, and what he could ask for help with, without fear of rejection or ridicule.

Mark chose to ask for help with the induction committee. He identified a couple of newer staff members who'd be able to bring new energy to the committee while freeing him up to not have to be at every meeting. At the right time, he'd be able to withdraw completely from the committee and leave it in their capable hands. With a sense of great relief and release, he decided that he would say no to the soccer coaching – with a wry chuckle, he admitted that there was a younger dad, with younger children, who'd been hinting that he'd like to take on the role. And he decided to say no to the guilt about not attending the art lectures – he realised that he was doing the course for his own interest and pleasure, so he gave himself permission to attend when he could and not worry when he couldn't. His shoulders literally relaxed in front of my eyes as he decided this.

By putting down what was no longer feeding him, Mark was able to not only spend more time running and doing more of what was good for him, but also make space for other, more appropriate people to pick up where he'd left off, which brought new energy into the soccer team and the induction committee – a win-win.

YOUR 'GOT DONE' LIST

We're often so focused on what we still have to do that we forget to acknowledge what we've already done. I guarantee that you're far more effective and productive than you give yourself credit for.

We feel overwhelmed by everything we need to do and worried that we'll never manage to finish everything – ever, let alone in the time we have available. Whenever we do manage to cross something off the list, we almost instantly replace it with two or three (or four or five) other items. We get so caught up in the pressure of striving to be more, do more, go further that we neglect to recognise and celebrate ourselves for what we've achieved.

Right now, in this moment, think about everything that you've managed to get done so far today, this week, this month and this year. Write it all down, from the little things ('I got to work without losing my temper in the traffic', 'I remembered to bring a healthy lunch for myself') to the big ones ('I submitted that assignment', 'I made that presentation', 'I landed that deal', I got that job or promotion').

Now pat yourself on the back.

And next time you're feeling overwhelmed and unproductive, look at this 'got done' list – or, even better, write another one.

Set your own agenda

Maintaining strong boundaries is very hard when we've become disconnected from ourselves and our inner world. When we've lost our internal and spiritual integrity, it's all too easy to surrender our own principles and priorities, and instead allow ourselves to be led by the needs or desires of others.

Kati experienced this with a job that demanded she do things she didn't want to do. Alicia experienced it when her life demanded she didn't do things she did want to do.

Alicia had always wanted to write a novel. At last, she'd managed to convert a room in her house into a study and everything was ready for her to start writing her masterpiece. But she just couldn't seem to find the time or the energy to go there. Every night she went to bed full of intentions to spend the next day at her computer, and every morning something more important came up. Her mother needed to be taken to the doctor (again). Her husband needed his lucky suit dry-cleaned. Her twins needed to be taken to a soccer match at the other end of town.

Alicia could barely remember to feed herself lunch, let alone find the enthusiasm to fire up her laptop. She was tired, tired, tired. She was tired of running around after everyone else. She was tired of meeting everyone's needs but her own. She was tired of never getting to do what she wanted to do. Alicia was starting to feel angry and resentful.

Like Alicia, many of us spend most of our waking hours thinking about others, listening to others and doing things for others. We drop whatever we're busy with to do whatever we're asked to by others. It's often only in the calm and quiet that descend when everyone else is asleep that we find the space to think about and remember our own needs and wants.

Those of us who have a close relationship with burnout are often more reactive than proactive. We tend to let the people around us set the agenda rather than sticking to our own plan – often to our detriment. If someone suggests something, we go along with it. If someone wants our help, we give it. This is partly because we aren't disciplined enough about identifying our own priorities but also because, as we know, we often struggle to say no. And we're inclined to put the needs and desires of others above our own – we're what I call 'others-centred'. And then we get to the end of the day and realise that we haven't achieved anything we promised ourselves we would. And the worst part is that we have no one to blame but ourselves.

It's imperative that we regularly and proactively identify what's important to us, and set goals and tasks that satisfy our own needs, wants and ambitions. And it isn't enough to just identify them – we need to honour them and make sure we make them happen.

If you make a plan, you're more likely to stick to it. If you know you have certain tasks that you want to accomplish every day/week/month, you'll be less likely to react to every request and demand from the people around you. If you sit down and proactively work out what you choose to spend your time and energy on, it'll be easier to say no to demands that don't suit or serve you. You'll be able to say, simply and calmly, that you're not available because you have other commitments.

YOUR DAILY CHECK-IN TOOL

This 10-minute daily check-in helps me to create my own agenda. I find it incredibly helpful and grounding to ask myself these questions. Give it a try – I think you will too!

What and how am I feeling today? Enthusiastic and excited.

Why do I feel this way today? I'm looking forward to working on my book and meeting the publishing team.

What do I want to do about it today? Enjoy my meetings and stay focused.

What do I want to do today? Work some more on the manuscript, meet the team, have tea with a friend, answer all emails.

What do I not want to do today? Waste time on social media, spend more than 30 minutes in total on the phone, eat sugar, forget to drink enough water, go to bed too late.

What do I want to have achieved by the end of the day? Another 45 pages of editing, all emails answered, eaten healthily, had a good meeting, enjoyed my time with my friend, gone for a walk with the dogs, enjoyed the evening with my family.

From always on to often off

If you're old enough, you may remember a time before smartphones – a time when work happened at work, and when we left work we left it. We'd get home in the late afternoon and know that we had hours of downtime stretching ahead of us. We could exercise, make a healthy supper (using fresh ingredients) that we would eat at the dinner table with our families while actually having a conversation about how our days had been. Then maybe we'd all gather around the TV and watch a show together as a family. We'd go to bed at a decent hour, maybe read a chapter or two of our books (real books, made of paper and ink) and then get a good night's sleep. In the mornings, we'd eat breakfast and then go to work and/or school, again having conversations with each other on our travels – face-to-face conversations, not phone conversations.

I'm deeply appreciative of modern technology and I love my smartphone, computer and Kindle.

But!

What technology gives with one virtual hand, it takes away with two or three others. Yes, we get to keep connected with friends all over the world. Yes, we get to have literally hundreds of books on one tiny device. Yes, we can make phone calls to family and friends and colleagues while we're driving.

And, yes, our virtual connections are limiting our actual connections.

No longer do we spend our evening commute leaving work behind while we drive towards home. Now, we take work with us on the journey and into the destination. We make phone calls from the car. Sometimes we even send emails from the car (when we're stopped at a red light, of course). There's no time and space to put down our work persona so that we can pick up our private persona. There are no clear boundaries between our professional and personal lives any more. Evenings and weekends now include answering emails, finalising reports and posting to social media. We look at our screens more than we look at each other.

Not only is our constant connectedness to our work and the outside world contributing enormously to our stress and feelings of being overwhelmed, it's also creating a disconnectedness from our lives and our inner worlds. We're on guard and ready for action all the time.

At any given waking hour, most of us are multitasking at a frightening rate – often without even being aware of it. We're responding to emails, reading text messages, catching up on the news and surfing social media and the net while we're in meetings, writing reports, watching TV, eating meals, having conversations, driving, walking, exercising – even bathing. And it's not as if the news and social media are full of good stories and uplifting posts. More often than not we're contaminating our minds and lives with horror stories, told by horror-mongers, of crazed political leaders, climate-change disasters and other news of death, disease, destruction and general discomfort. It's crazy.

Constantly tuning in to ambient messages and signals leaves us feeling frizzled and frazzled. It isn't natural or sustainable. Yet so many of us seem to do it. We're constantly on alert, ready for action, waiting to do whatever is expected of us.

To be always on is nice if you're a coffee shop or an airport, but pretty draining and exhausting if you're a human being. We need to learn how to flip the switch from always on to often off.

When I was at school, I was fascinated to learn about the movement of solvents through semipermeable membranes during osmosis. I love the concept of a *semipermeable* membrane – a membrane permeable enough to allow certain molecules to flow through it but not permeable enough to let everything through.

I like to think of our boundaries as semipermeable membranes. Good, healthy boundaries allow positive energy to flow into our lives while keeping negative energy out. They also allow the release of negative energy while protecting the positive energy from leaking away.

We get burnout when our boundaries are too permeable – when we allow in everything, good and bad; when we can't keep anything in, good or bad. When our energy field is like a beach, with a sea of other people's energies washing over,

49

into, out of and around us, slowly our own energy gets washed away, just like the sand on the beach.

Sometimes when we have burnout we go to the opposite extreme. We're so worn out and exhausted that we build big solid walls to keep out the bad. Sadly, this not only keeps out the good, but it also keeps in the bad.

We need to develop boundaries that allow in the good and keep it in, and that allow out the bad and keep it out. This takes time and mindfulness.

CUT OUT UNNECESSARY INTERFERENCE

Every day we all experience numerous interruptions to and intrusions on our time and energy. A buzzing phone, a pinging email inbox and social-media alerts all become annoying invasions that not only impact negatively on our productivity but can also leave us feeling fragmented and dis-integrated. Tighten up your boundaries by reducing the interruptions and irritations that you allow into your space.

Here are some ideas for reducing irritations:

❋ Go through your email inbox and delete unwanted subscriptions.

❋ Cancel newsletters and notifications that don't add any value.

❋ Opt out of spam text messages (they'll just keep sending them otherwise).

❋ Disable social-media notifications on your smartphone.

❋ Unfriend or unfollow people who post negative or offensive things.

❋ Better yet, remove all social media and email apps from your smartphone — less of the smart and more of the phone!

❋ Set time aside for social media and email correspondence every day, and don't go there until the designated time.

❋ Leave your phone behind when you go out with friends or into a meeting.

TAKE PROPER BREAKS

Perhaps the most destructive habit of busy people is eating lunch at our desks while we continue to work, read the news on social media, or try to balance the household budget.

When you have your lunch or tea break at your desk or in front of your computer or while busy on your smartphone, you swallow the stress and anxiety that comes up in response to what you're reading. You're not doing yourself any favours when you eat your sandwich over your keyboard.

A useful and healthy break doesn't have to be long, but it does need to be total. Ten minutes in the sun away from your worries and in the fresh air is much more beneficial than an hour in front of your computer. Ingesting clean air along with your food is so much healthier than swallowing the woes of the world as you swallow your lunch.

When you need to take a break, step away from your desk.

Reconnect with all your relationships

Its 10pm and Siya has only just got back to his room in the student residence he stays in – 14 hours after he left it this morning. All he wants is a good night's sleep, but he still has to make and eat supper and have a shower, by which time he knows he'll be overtired and will struggle to get to sleep. The thought of lying awake for hours, worrying about all the work he hasn't managed to complete, is terrifying. He knows he'll be exhausted tomorrow and struggle to concentrate in class, which means he'll have to go to the library all evening to try and make sense of what he couldn't get to grips with during the day. This pattern has been going on for some weeks now and it's making him feel a little desperate.

Most days, the constant demand of preparing for class discussions, tests, assignments and exams feels oppressive and relentless. He spends all his time working and worrying about work, and is spending less and less time with his friends and family. He lives on his own, the course he's studying demands a lot of individual work, and he's too exhausted and stressed to play social sports at the moment. As well as being stressed, exhausted, overwhelmed and anxious, Siya is isolated and lonely. He's starting to feel that he hates his life and can't remember why he signed up to be an engineer anyway.

Siya is far from unique. Student support programmes are increasingly concerned about the alarming rise in stress, anxiety and depression, and even suicide, among students, in South Africa in particular but also elsewhere in the world. Being young is no guarantee that you won't fall prey to burnout.

One of the most worrying aspects of the overload that our students are exhibiting is a retreat from social interactions in an attempt to get on top of their academic responsibilities. They turn down invitations to have meals with their families (if they live close enough to get there easily and affordably) because they have 'too much work to do'. They spend less and less time with their friends and more and more time on their own in the library. It's no wonder that so many students are lonely and depressed. They're right back down at the bottom of Maslow's hierarchy of needs.

Psychologist Abraham Maslow's hierarchy of needs starts with the most basic: food, water, shelter and warmth. The next level of needs that must be met are those relating to safety and security: physical safety, financial security, health and wellbeing. The third level is that of love and belonging: friends, intimacy and family. Level four is esteem: self-esteem and self-respect, and the esteem and respect of others. And right at the top is self-actualisation: understanding what our full potential is and being able to reach it.

We all know that relationships (whether they're intimate, platonic or familial) are essential to meet our needs of belonging, acceptance and community. But when we're burned out, our relationships get moved down the list of things to pay attention to and put effort into. Like Siya, when we're in survival mode, there's little or no time to thrive socially or romantically. It's all we can do to ensure that we're taking care of our physiological and safety needs; we meet the bare minimum of the requirements of our lives and hope that everything else will take care of itself.

We start to pull back from our communities and our social circles. At first, we put less effort into the people and pastimes on the periphery of our lives. As we get more and more exhausted and overwhelmed, we pull in our energy more and our social circle gets smaller and smaller. If we don't pay attention to the burnout, that circle gets so small that our energy and attention are focused on just getting ourselves through the day. We're so busy just holding it together that we forget to pay attention to our relationships. And it's our relationships more than anything else that make our experience of and in the world meaningful. (And, by the way, I believe that we have relationships with more than just other people; we form meaningful bonds with pets, hobbies, books, art and plenty of other pastimes.)

We need to reconnect with people and practices that are important to us and that feed our soul, because then we'll be reconnecting with what's important and meaningful to and for ourselves.

REACH OUT AND RECONNECT

In the midst of your exhaustion, you may have found yourself withdrawing from some relationships or pastimes.

In some cases, this may be a positive development for you as you may have withdrawn from seeing people or doing things that drain your energy or make you feel bad about yourself. In other cases, this withdrawal may not be so positive. Perhaps you miss a person or activity. Maybe you don't laugh as much or have as much fun in their absence. Maybe you're feeling lonely and isolated. Perhaps you miss the companionship of taking your dog for a walk. Maybe you miss the rush of creating a new painting.

Now is the time to think about who or what may be missing from your life as a result of your burnout, and take steps to bring them back. Identify one or two relationships that you haven't been paying enough attention to lately. Contact a person you miss; send a message, make a phone call, arrange to meet for a coffee. Go for a walk with the dog, take yourself to an art gallery, read a favourite book.

It doesn't really matter what you do, but do something to enrich your life and to make you feel more of a sense of love and belonging.

RECONNECT BY ASKING FOR HELP

A straightforward way to rekindle relationships and enhance connections is to ask for help. Often a difficult thing to do, it can be especially hard to ask for help when we have burnout. This is partly because we've become so withdrawn and focused on our own survival that it doesn't even occur to us that we can ask for help. And it's partly because we're already feeling so vulnerable that we can't risk the rejection that asking for help may bring.

But I firmly believe that we risk rejection by *not* asking for help. In their book *Receiving Love*, Harville Hendrix and Helen LaKelly Hunt write that when our relationships start to get a bit tricky and not as satisfying as we'd like them to be, most of us respond by trying to *give* more. But, they suggest, what we should be doing to heal our relationships is to *receive* more. Instead of doing more for others, we should be allowing them to do more for us. When we don't allow people to help us, we're rejecting their offers of support, and it often feels like we're rejecting them. If you don't believe me, think about the last time an offer of help you made was rejected and remember how it felt.

Asking for help from people who will be willing and able to give it is a very powerful way of establishing, or re-establishing, social contact. When we allow ourselves to ask for and accept help, we're allowing our relationships to grow and flourish. Offers and actions of help and support are acts of love. When we let people help us, we're letting them love us.

If it feels too hard to start at home, start with a stranger. Instead of looking for something in the supermarket, you could ask one of the staff members to show you where to find it; instead of driving around lost, you could ask someone for directions…

ASK FOR HELP

No one can do everything all by themselves. All that happens when we try to do everything, be everything, need nothing and need no one is that we exhaust ourselves and alienate everyone around us.

I have no doubt that there are many things that you can do excellently and I'm equally sure that there are at least some things that you're not so good at. Luckily, we're all different and we all have different strengths and weaknesses. So the things you may struggle with, the person sitting next to you might be brilliant at.

Have a look at your to-do list and identify the items that you know other people would be able to do better than you and/or help you to do better. Now identify who those other people are. And you know what to do next …

It takes courage and strength to ask for help. And it often takes generosity too. We have to be brave enough and strong enough to show that we're not perfect. We have to be generous enough to give someone else an opportunity to grow and shine.

Get more rest

'Sleep is for the weak.' 'I'll sleep when I'm dead.' 'I'm too busy to sleep.'

These days, it seems that getting by on the bare minimum of rest is a badge of honour. Really, it's enough to make this burnout-recovery coach want to weep (once I've finished gnashing my teeth).

If you tell yourself you'll sleep when you're dead, you're going to be dead a lot sooner than you think! In this age of 'having it all', it can be hard to say no to being busier and yes to getting more rest – but having it all comes at a price. Countless studies have shown that not getting enough sleep is extremely harmful to our short-, medium- and long-term health. The UK's National Health Service advises that regular poor sleep puts us at risk of serious medical conditions including obesity, heart disease and diabetes, and shortens our life expectancy.

If we keep burning the candle at both ends, there'll be nothing left to burn. And if we keep stretching ourselves too far, we'll snap. I know this because I see the results of overwork and under-rest every day in my coaching practice.

You need to plan to spend your time and energy wisely. You can start to do this immediately by getting more sleep. Because the more sleep you get, the more effective you'll become.

TIME TO GO TO BED

It takes much longer to prepare for bed than we think it does. Just as our computers need to close all programmes and applications before they can shut down, we also need to finish off what we're busy with before we can go to sleep.

It takes time to create the calm and quiet environment necessary for easy sleep. If you want to be asleep by 10pm, you probably need to start the shutting-down process by 9pm at the latest. Stop whatever it is you're doing (looking at all screens, listening to music, thinking about work, eating or drinking) and start your bedtime routine (locking the house, washing, brushing teeth, getting into sleep clothes, turning off the lights …). By the time you have finished shutting down and switching off, it will be 10pm and you will be ready for a good, and long, night's sleep.

HAVE LUNCH WITH SOMEONE

I know: you're busy, you're stressed, you've got a deadline, you either need to have lunch at your computer today, even though you know you shouldn't, or you can only spare 10 minutes to eat.

Don't do that to yourself.

Give your lunch the attention it deserves – and that includes finding someone to connect with while you're eating. If a trouble shared is a trouble halved, then a pleasure shared is a pleasure doubled.

MAINTAIN YOUR
STRENGTH

4

Burnout isn't one thing

Burnout isn't just a feeling of exhaustion, being overwhelmed, and being extremely stressed and anxious. It's not merely feeling tired all the time, not wanting to see friends and having no appetite for anything other than sugar, carbs and caffeine. It isn't only feeling stretched in too many different and competing directions, by too many different and competing demands. It's not simply a result of struggling to say no or failing to ask for help.

It's all these things and more. It's also a feeling of listlessness and ineptitude, a lack of enthusiasm and excitement, an existential emergency.

Burnout is a complex and systemic condition. Each element and aspect of burnout is connected to and influenced by every other element and aspect. The social aspects are connected to the emotional aspects, which are connected to the physical aspects, which are connected to the professional aspects and the financial aspects, and the domestic aspects, and the environmental aspects, and any other aspects you can think of.

That's why just paying attention to the physical pieces of the puzzle isn't enough to solve the problem. Eating more fruit and fewer chocolates is a good start, but it isn't going to deal with the conditions that gave rise to the bad eating habits in the first place. Reducing stress levels (and, as I've often said, if anyone can tell me how to do that, I'd be very grateful) is a great ambition but doesn't interrogate the underlying traits and thoughts that generate the stress.

The fact is that we're part of a complex ecosystem and our burnout is a component of the larger whole.

Keeping our personal ecosystems healthy

Ecology is the branch of biology that studies how organisms – including people – relate to each other and their environment. There are many tiny elements in an ecosystem that are all interrelated and that all affect and are affected by each other. If one element in the ecosystem is working too hard or not hard enough, the whole system is altered. In a lake, for instance, if the delicate balance of light, water, air, sand, plants, fish, frogs and ducks is destabilised by a drought, the lack of rain leads to overcrowding in the water, which results in moss and other plant life dying and decomposing, using up precious oxygen. The lower levels of oxygen result in the suffocation of the fish, which results in the starvation of the frogs and ducks, which results in the increase in the numbers of pests like snails and slugs…

The health of any ecosystem, be it in the natural world or in our own private world, depends on all the various parts that make up the system maintaining their equilibrium. Our survival is dependent on the health and balance of the ecosystems that we're part of. We're affected by all the various elements that make up our own personal ecosystems, from our own innate biology and nature and what they require, to our families, our work, the communities we're a part of, the society and country we live in, and even the world at large... We're very much part of a greater whole.

If one element of the whole is out of balance, it has a knock-on effect on all the other elements of the system. What may start off as a small unhappiness in one life area (say, work) can soon spill over into other life areas. And, left unchecked, that unhappiness can start to affect the whole of life. Burnout results when our ecosystem gets out of balance and, rather than working together to support each other, one or more elements start to work against each other.

If we want to recover and stay recovered from burnout, we need to ensure that the health and equilibrium of our ecosystem is restored.

CUMULATIVE BURNOUT

When Grace arrived for her first coaching session with me, she was so emotionally bruised and battered that I wasn't sure if I could help her or if I should refer her to a psychologist for depression. A very petite and extremely thin woman, she was obviously very anxious and looked as though she may spontaneously combust at any moment. As jittery as a deer walking past a lions' den, she could barely sit still and talked nineteen to the dozen.

She was a few months into a job she hated, doing meaningless work with people she didn't respect for an organisation that was fraught with conflict. The job also entailed a lot of travel, which meant she was away from home a couple of nights a week.

Grace was in a relationship with a man who had turned blowing hot and cold into an Olympic sport. Her mother was frail and needy, and demanded a lot of Grace's attention and precious free time. Most of her friends were coupled up, and spending too much time with them served only to rub salt into her wounds.

She lived in a complex that attracted lots of young professionals and should have been a lovely place to live, but instead Grace felt assaulted by the loud parties her neighbours held every Friday and Saturday night and most Sundays in the daytime. Her home wasn't the place of refuge she so desperately needed. She wasn't sleeping enough, and she was too worn out to make sure she was eating properly or exercising well.

To add to all her stress, Grace was keenly interested in current affairs, and watched or read any source of news and commentary she could find time for. The constant stream of information about politics, corruption, crime, instability and uncertainty only added to her already unhealthy sense of doom and gloom.

Any one of those challenges would have been enough to send Grace into the burnout danger zone, but simultaneously combined, they gave her no chance of escaping unscathed. What Grace had was a perfect example of what I call 'cumulative burnout'. At almost every level, and in almost every sphere of her life, she was experiencing exhaustion, helplessness and hopelessness. It was a perfect storm of pain, stress and unhappiness.

Once she'd expended enough nervous energy to calm down and be present with herself and with me, I asked her to complete a 'wheel of life' exercise. This is a powerful way to identify where life is good and where it needs to be improved. Grace's wheel showed that, while she was pleased with the amount of money she earned and with her personal growth (she was studying part-time to further her qualifications), the other areas of her life were not even satisfactory, let alone making her happy.

The 'wheel of life' exercise helps us to quickly and easily identify where we're out of balance so that we can take steps to regain some equilibrium in our lives. When you draw your own wheel of life, you'll probably notice, as most people do, the interrelatedness of your satisfaction, or lack thereof, in the different areas – for instance, you may find that the good money you earn comes at the expense of doing work that's not right for you, or that what 'me' time you have may be impacted by your physical or social environment.

While scoring a perfect 10 in each of the life areas would be fabulous, it's not realistic. The aim is to get the wheel as round and balanced as possible, so that our lives feel and become more steady and stable. We're aiming for even scores rather than high scores; and high even scores are the ultimate goal, reflective of a healthy and happy ecosystem.

YOUR WHEEL OF LIFE

Make your own wheel of life to see where your life is out of balance, and think about the changes you need to make in order to ensure the wheel is rounder and more in balance.

Draw a circle on a page. Divide the circle into eight so that it looks like a bicycle wheel. Label each of the eight sections of this wheel to represent the main areas of your life.

1. Work
2. Personal growth
3. Physical environment (micro and macro)
4. Intimate relationships
5. Relationships with family and friends
6. Money
7. 'Me' time
8. Health (good and bad, including sleep, eating, rest, exercise, drinking, smoking, etc.)

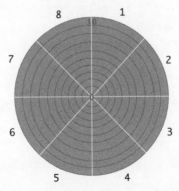

Allocate a score between 0 (very unhappy, at the centre of the wheel) and 10 (very happy, on the outer rim) to illustrate your current level of satisfaction in each area of your life, and mark the appropriate place on the 'spoke' of the wheel.

Now ask yourself:

❋ If this was a wheel on your car, how smooth would your ride through life be?

❋ Which life areas have you identified as being less than satisfactory?

❋ Which areas are you satisfied with?

Now identify two or three goals or resolutions for each of the life areas, either to improve things that are already working for you, or to address things that aren't.

CHANGE YOUR SPACE

Take a look around you right now. How is the physical space you find yourself in *reflecting* how you're feeling, and/or how may it be *affecting* how you're feeling?

Is there a pile of clutter that's making you feel anxious and out of control, or are your feelings of being overwhelmed and out of control being reflected by the mess on your desk? Is the noise in your head making you more aware of the noise around you, or is the noise in your environment negatively affecting your stress and anxiety levels? Are the flowers on the dresser making you happy, or did your happiness make you buy some flowers for your dresser?

Our inner and outer worlds are mirrors of each other. It can be hard to know what comes first.

What I do know (and I'm sure you do too) is that making a positive change to your space results in a positive change in your spirit.

Choose one thing that you can do right now to improve your space. Tidy up, throw away old magazines and burned-out candles, wash the windows, stick up a picture that makes you happy.

Even a tiny change to what you see can make a big change to how you feel.

5

You and your Survivor Self

I'm often asked by journalists to give advice on various articles. I get asked to comment on questions like 'Why do women have affairs with married men?' or 'What makes people push themselves too hard?' Wouldn't it be nice if I could answer those questions! Instead, I explain that the only way to get any accurate insights would be to ask every single woman having an affair with a married man, or every single person who drives themself too hard.

Everybody is unique, and we all have unique circumstances and contexts that determine our responses to the world around us, so it's impossible to reach an absolute understanding of the choices that all people make. It is, I believe, disrespectful to presume to know what makes every person tick, to ascribe blanket reasons for actions and choices.

That said, there are certain less-than-helpful thoughts and beliefs and actions I've begun to identify in myself and in my clients. Why do we engage in restrictive habits? What is the reason for the sometimes self-abusive choices we make? This is how my concept of the Survivor Self was born.

Where does the Survivor Self come from?

Our Survivor Self is the part of us that has looked after us and ensured that we've got to where we are now. It's specific to our experiences and has its own distinct way of getting us through life, picking up all sorts of unconscious beliefs, ideas and coping mechanisms along the way.

Every single one of us is unique, and so is our interaction with the world around us. Millions of people may share a common difficulty (for instance, with establishing and keeping a healthy relationship, or maintaining a healthy lifestyle), but each one of us has a different set of beliefs, experiences, expectations and behaviours that combine to make our circumstances specific to us. Whether our challenges relate to love, work, food, alcohol or anything else, we all have our own way of understanding and responding to what's going on in our lives.

Each of us has developed a set of responses, adaptations and adjustments that have (or haven't) helped us to navigate our way through disappointments, fears and successes. We've made sense of all the good and all the bad things that have happened to and around us, and incorporated that meaning into a set of unconscious expectations, beliefs and behaviours that determine how we are in the world.

This is all embodied in the Survivor Self, the unconscious but very powerful part of us that's motivated by a desire to keep us safe. When we were children, our Survivor Self stepped in when we felt under threat and when things felt too big and scary for us to manage and make sense of. The harm we feared may have been real or imagined, small or severe. Whatever the scale and extent, it *felt* scary and dangerous at the time – and as though our very survival was under threat.

The Survivor Self did what it felt it needed to do to keep us alive, for instance by keeping us safe and cared for by taking care of everyone around us. We started to look after others in the way that we wanted to be looked after ourselves: we tried to do anything we could to make it easier for our parents/caregivers to love us, becoming very reliable and responsible, or taking on adult duties like cooking, cleaning or childcare in the family, or working very hard at school and/or taking on paying jobs at a very early age.

Our Survivor Self may have witnessed dysfunctional relationships and developed an expectation of similar dysfunction in our own relationships. Or it may have experienced the disappointment of feeling undervalued and unappreciated, and incorporated that experience into a desire to protect us from more disappointment.

Just as we all have different experiences and observations, so the expectations and fears that drive our Survivor Self are different for everyone. One person's Survivor Self may protect their person by not getting too invested in a job or a relationship or a hobby, while another person's Survivor Self may work by making their person become overly invested – even if the investment in that job or person or pastime is unhealthy.

Your current Survivor Self

The strategies your Survivor Self may have adopted were probably very effective when you were small (otherwise you may not be reading this right now) but the thoughts and behaviours that helped to keep you feeling safe when you were a child may no longer be the best thing for you now that you're a grownup – and they may even be contributing to your burnout.

Your Survivor Self may be the part of you that struggles to say no and to ask for help. It may be the reason why you take on more than you can handle, why you don't have clear boundaries and/or why you feel compelled to meet everyone else's needs and wants at the expense of your own happiness and wellbeing.

Remember Alicia, who was trying to write her book while at the beck and call of everyone around her? Alicia is the eldest of three children. Her younger brother

69

and sister are twins who were born when she was 7. Their father couldn't manage the stress of twin newborns and abandoned the family, leaving Alicia with an exhausted, overwhelmed and very sad single mother. Alicia quickly learned that if she wanted any degree of harmony at home, she needed to help – a lot. She'd help change nappies and give bottles, and warm up her own ready-made meals in the microwave when her mom was asleep or busy with the babies.

One of the unconscious (and therefore very powerful) beliefs that Alicia's Survivor Self developed was 'I have to help wherever I can'. Is it any wonder that she drops everything she's busy with as soon as someone asks her for help? Her Survivor Self is the driving force behind her trying to support everyone around her – often at her own expense.

If, for any of a number of reasons, we feel that the adults aren't doing a good enough job of looking after us, we may unconsciously start to believe that we need to look after the grownups so that they can look after us – just as Alicia did. Our child-minds tell us that the only way we can be cared for the way we need to be cared for, is to look after our caregivers so that they can look after us.

For Sipho, who filled all his waking hours being busy even though what he was busy with exhausted and isolated him, one of his Survivor Self beliefs was 'I need to be seen to be remembered' – which sadly became a self-fulfilling prophecy the more he withdrew from his friends.

With some compassionate coaching, Alicia and Sipho were able to put words to their Survivor Self beliefs (well, at least some of them) and then to update them so that they were a truer and more accurate reflection of their current reality. Alicia's 'I have to help wherever I can' was amended to 'I can choose how to help', and Sipho revised his belief to the truer 'When I remember myself I am not forgotten about'.

Survivor Self beliefs develop from real experiences. They felt (and quite possibly were) real when you were a child. But they're most probably not still real or true now that you're an adult. It's extremely powerful and liberating to identify what some of our Survivor Self strategies may have been and/or continue to be, so that we can understand how they may be contributing to our burnout. When you identify and name your Survivor Self beliefs and strategies, you'll be able to update them to reflect your current, empowered reality. Then you can move away from surviving and start thriving.

UPDATING YOUR SURVIVOR SELF

Think back to when you were a child. Try and identify the kinds of Survivor Self strategies (they may be habits, behaviours or beliefs) that you developed as a way to feel safe and secure in your world. You may, for instance, avoid conflict because of an idea that it's imperative that everyone around you is happy and not angry or disappointed.

Now think about if there are any connections between those habits, behaviours or beliefs and your current levels of energy, exhaustion or feelings of being overwhelmed. For instance, that need for everyone to be happy and not angry may be causing you to go out of your way to give your family and friends everything you think they need or want. Another example is a compulsion to be noticed and appreciated at work that may be driving you to put in too many hours. Or you could be harbouring a fear that if you don't look after people, something terrible may happen to them, and that could be pushing you to be over-responsible, causing exhaustion and resentment.

If you're able to identify some Survivor Self strategies that are no longer serving you, perhaps you can consciously choose new ones to replace them? You can start by asking yourself if those statements are still true and still necessary. If they are neither, then try to identify a strategy that's more appropriate for you right now. Maybe you can allow yourself to say no to something or someone, safe in the knowledge that whatever may ensue won't devastate you — because you're a grownup, adult, strong person now.

FEELGOODS

A feelgood is exactly what it sounds like: something that makes you feel good. Feelgoods are very good at counterbalancing all of the many and varied things that make us feel not so good.

It's useful to have a 'catalogue' of feelgoods that we can look at and choose from when we need calming down, cheering up or getting over something. The simpler and easier your catalogue is to use, the better.

Identify as many of the things that make you feel good as possible (you can keep adding to it), and write them down in a special place. To help you get started, you can think about things you love to eat, to drink, to smell, to touch, to hear; people you love to see and speak to; books and passages you love to read; songs or music you love to listen to; experiences you love to have; and places you love to go.

Now choose one feelgood and make it happen for yourself, right now.

Doesn't that feel good?

The struggle was real

South Africa has a long and troubled history of social, political and economic injustice and inequality. The last couple of decades of apartheid were brutal, and the last few years particularly so, with the National Party declaring States of Emergency in a desperate attempt to stop the inevitable social and political change.

In the late 1980s and early 1990s, anti-apartheid activists around the country spent many hours planning awareness-raising events, protesting various atrocities committed by the state, getting into running battles with the teargas- and rubber-bullet-wielding riot police, and looking over their shoulders for the omnipresent security police. The sense of outrage and the fury they felt with the government of the day was matched only by the fear and dread they felt of the security forces, the constant anxiety that they were being followed and their phone conversations being listened to, or that they'd be picked up by the police and taken away without the knowledge of their families and friends. Anti-apartheid activists and their loved ones were always especially aware of the threat of the particularly ruthless detention without trial.

Apartheid ended more than 25 years ago, but for many South Africans, the internal struggle is still in evidence. Many of my clients are recovering from the bad old years of apartheid and the struggle to end it.

STATES OF EMERGENCY
'I can't stop feeling as though it'll be a total and utter disaster if I don't finish things in time. I feel like I have to be available to troubleshoot for all of my colleagues – and my family and friends – 24/7. If there's a problem, I feel like I need to attend to it immediately. I feel like I'm on high alert all the time.' A tear rolls down Brenda's face. 'And I'm just so very, very tired.'

Back in the bad old days, Brenda was a student activist – someone who prioritised raising awareness of and protesting against the many tyrannies of the apartheid government. Those of us who lived through those crazy, terrifying, exhilarating years can relate to Brenda and her ongoing battle to find a place of peace and rest within herself. The constant sense of impending doom and the need to right every wrong we see or hear about is still present. The feeling that everything we're asked or expected to do is urgent and critical is a hangover from when we were living under a State of Emergency where everything really was an emergency. Now it feels like an emergency even if it isn't one.

We struggle with boundaries, with knowing when to stop, with knowing who to trust and who to be wary of. We struggle with knowing how to discern what needs to happen now and what can wait. So, like Brenda, we push ourselves to finish whatever we start as soon as we start it – because what if we get taken away by the baddies while we're in the middle of something? It will never be finished and we'll be letting down everyone around us.

We feel like we have to do whatever is asked of us, help whoever needs it as soon as they request it – because what if we don't help someone and they're taken away and interrogated and/or tortured and/or maybe even killed? We'll be responsible.

We also feel like we need to do everything well, discreetly and without drawing attention to ourselves – because what if by asking for help we draw attention to what we're doing and put ourselves and everyone else in danger? We'll be responsible for that too.

Back then, our Survivor Self stepped up and rose to the challenge of keeping us, and everyone around us, safe. But that was then and this is now. Thankfully, we don't live in a State of Emergency any more. We can put down the sense of life-or-death that accompanied us then, and replace it with a calmer and more measured approach to how we do (or don't do) things.

SUCCEEDER GUILT

Brenda, and many like her, also endure what I call 'succeeder guilt', a slightly more complex version of survivor guilt that drives certain people to try to make up for all the things the people around them don't have, or don't have enough of.

Many people who lived through the struggle and managed to build a life for themselves post-1990 bear a certain level of guilt related to coming out alive and being able to get on with building careers and families. They survived, while many of their peers, friends and loved ones weren't so lucky. Twenty-something years into democracy, our country and its people are still suffering from varying degrees of Post-Traumatic Stress Disorder (PTSD) and survivor guilt, with, for many of us, an added dose of contrition about having more than others.

We may have more opportunities for education and employment than our parents and grandparents, who were born in a different time. We may have more success than peers, siblings and cousins. We may have more money and material comfort than friends and family, with nicer houses and cars. We may have happier relationships and more accomplished children. We may have more fulfilling work. The list is almost endless. Anything that we have that others don't can make us feel guilty. And the larger the gap between what we have and what others don't, the larger the guilt.

Succeeder guilt is another reason so many of my clients develop burnout. They stay in jobs they hate because their salary is contributing to the survival and wellbeing of countless members of their extended families. They obtain degrees and follow career paths that feel meaningless because they're trying to compensate for the education and job opportunities that those who went before them never had access to. They live a life that isn't of their choice because they're constantly aware of how lucky they are and how much was sacrificed by so many for them to get to where they are now.

Although succeeder guilt is particularly prevalent among people who are the first in their families to be born after political turmoil and strife, or to make it through university, I think that it's something that can afflict anyone with any degree of compassion, sensitivity and empathy towards the experiences of those who have gone before them in life. In a world where material disparities are growing, not only in size but also in evidence, it's hard for people who are alert to the plight of those less fortunate to allow themselves to feel truly and wholly worthy of their success and comfort. The cognitive dissonance that results when we know we've worked hard for everything we've achieved, but we still feel guilty about having more than others, is very emotionally taxing and can keep us stuck doing things that are bad for us so that we're able to assuage our guilt.

The combination of a sense of impending emergency or crisis and succeeder guilt is a particularly nasty and powerful cocktail that fuels and exacerbates the development of burnout. We need to release ourselves from their intoxicating effects if we're to ensure that future generations are free of them.

CUT YOURSELF SOME SLACK

If you're an adult child or experience succeeder guilt, you're probably very hard on yourself and judge yourself without mercy. Nothing you do ever feels quite good enough and you always feel you could do better – despite what everyone else tells you. You constantly put yourself under pressure to try harder, do more, be the best; to not show weakness, not ask for help, never take a break – no matter how needed and well-deserved.

And how's that working out for you?

My guess is you're tired, depleted, anxious and stressed. Because when we're in the 'if I were better, it would be better' frame of mind, what's good enough is a constantly moving target, and constant, unrelenting pressure to try harder, achieve more, do better, and be better sucks all the joy and enjoyment out of what we do. If we can't allow ourselves to recognise what we achieve and how well we achieve it, what's the point of even trying?

Nobody is perfect. No one gets everything right all the time. Not even you. Allow yourself to acknowledge your achievements, to recognise jobs well done, to make mistakes, to need help, to feel cross, to be sad.

STOP MULTITASKING

Our instinct when we're busy is to try to do more than one thing at once – return phone calls while in the car, edit reports while in a meeting, check emails while we're on a call. Multitasking is very fragmenting, distracting and dis-integrating. We aren't fully present in any of the tasks, and we're doing none of them (or ourselves) the justice they deserve.

6

Others-centredness

Alicia's Survivor Self belief that she had to help wherever she could laid the foundation for her others-centredness. The propensity to do things for others at our own expense is what I call being 'others-centred', and I believe it's at the root of much of the burnout I see all around me. We're others-centred when we put everyone else in the centre of our lives, and ourselves on the periphery. We're others-centred when we suspend our own priorities to meet the demands of others.

When we're others-centred we spend all our energy outside of ourselves. We put other people's needs (be they real or imagined) first, and our own needs last. We're so concerned with the wellbeing of others that we forget how to be well ourselves. We find ourselves meeting everyone else's needs and not our own. And then we get to the end of the day or the week or the month or the year and realise that we haven't achieved the things we identified as being important for us to achieve.

We are the afterword in our own stories.

Others-centredness is a bad habit and some of us have had it for a very long time – probably since we were children. It may have started off as a desire to please a parent and get rewarded – you ate the spinach you hated so that you could have the ice cream you loved. It probably evolved to wanting to fit in and be accepted – you wore the 'right' clothes to attract the attention of the guy or girl you had a crush on. You may even have started to smoke and drink to impress others.

When you got married you found yourself spending time with your spouse's family and friends – even the ones you didn't like very much. As a parent, you may find yourself listening to your kids' music in the car just to keep the peace.

Your others-centredness has evolved and developed over time, just as you have. What started off as a desire to show love can progress into a compulsion to try to ensure that you are loved.

Of course, it's all unconscious and we don't even know that we're doing it most of the time. We're oblivious to the fact that we turn ourselves inside-out and upside-down in our attempts to look after other people – all in the hope that they will look after us in return.

The problem, though, is that in our quest to look after others, we not only neglect to look after ourselves, but we also make it impossible for others to look after us in return – even though that's exactly what we crave.

Being all things to all people becomes ingrained in our thoughts and actions, and we forget to think about what we need to be to ourselves. We don't ask for help because we don't think about ourselves for long enough to realise that we need help. We don't say no to anyone in case we upset them or let them down. And we most certainly don't put ourselves first. Or second. Or even third.

When we consistently put ourselves last (even if we aren't asked to do so) we end up angry, resentful and burned out. Our health suffers, our self-esteem suffers and, ironically, our relationships suffer. When we start to realise that we've forgotten to remember ourselves, we start to get angry with the people we did remember. And that's what was starting to happen with Alicia, who was becoming so resentful towards everyone around her that she was, quite frankly, horrible to be around.

The Cs

The 5 Cs is a tool I created to help people like Alicia to think through how they want to respond to the various demands being made on them. Whether those demands are outright requests for assistance or more subtle demands of living or working with difficult people, the 5 Cs – clarity, choice, commitment, consequences and communication – help clarify the healthy path ahead.

1. CLARITY

We start off by getting clear on what's going on: who wants what, and what the bigger picture is. It helps to take a step back and try to understand what's happening objectively – as an observer rather than a participant.

When Alicia started thinking about her dissatisfaction, she was able to see that she'd been feeling angry and resentful because she ensured that everyone else got what they desired but she didn't ever seem to get what she wanted. She was able to recognise that an unfortunate dynamic (of which she was a part) had developed that required her to do whatever anyone asked of her, whenever they asked it. There was an increasing expectation of Alicia that she would be available and willing to do the bidding of anyone and everyone around her.

She was also able to recognise that her Survivor Self belief ('I have to help wherever I can') was the driving force behind much of the discomfort she found herself experiencing. It was the reason she picked up the dry-cleaning, ferried her mother and children wherever they wanted to go, and acceded to any other last-minute unscheduled demand. It was also the reason she never even considered the possibility of asking for help or saying no.

2. CHOICE

Armed with newfound clarity, Alicia spent some time thinking about how she, from a calm and rational space, would like to respond to all the demands being made on her. She realised that she could choose – not only if she was going to say yes or no, but also how she could agree to assist. After careful reflection, Alicia decided that she would continue to assist and support her family, but that the assistance and support would happen only after she'd helped herself by making space to do her writing in the mornings. She resolved that she would spend four hours every day (from 9am to 1pm) in her study, working on her book. She wouldn't be available for anything or anyone else (other than real emergencies, obviously) during those hours. After 1pm, she'd be free to help where and how she could and chose to.

3. COMMITMENT

Alicia made a commitment to herself that she would block off those four hours every day of the working week and wouldn't consider any requests for assistance during that time – no coffee dates, no fetching and carrying people, and even no answering the phone for chats with friends. The hours between 9am and 1pm were kept strictly for writing. She took this commitment to herself one step further by talking to her family and friends about her decision, and getting their agreement to support her. In this way, she contracted with others to respect her writing time and to not interrupt her or ask her for help during those hours.

4. CONSEQUENCES

As we know, the road to hell (and burnout) is paved with good intentions, and we suspected it was going to be hard for Alicia to stick to the commitment she'd made to herself. Our concern was that she may abandon her plan as soon as someone asked her to, or as soon as anyone got angry and pushed back against her new regime. So I asked her to think through what the possible consequences (good and bad) might be if she both did and didn't honour her commitment.

Thinking through possible consequences is possibly the most important of the five steps, because forewarned is forearmed. Alicia was able to anticipate what may happen when she stuck to her commitment (her family may be cross with her, they may call her selfish, she'd feel guilty... *and* she would get to write her book, she wouldn't be so resentful any more, her boundaries would be better, her relationships would be healthier...). Thinking about what she might experience if she didn't stick to her commitment (she wouldn't have her own time, she'd never write her book, her resentment would grow, her relationships would be compromised…) also helped her to be even more resolute about sticking to it.

5. COMMUNICATION

Alicia needed to give her family some notice so that they could get used to the idea and stop making appointments or plans that involved Alicia between 9am and 1pm. How was she going to do this? She spoke to her family, individually and together, and explained that from a certain date, she would be keeping office hours of 9am to 1pm and wouldn't be available to help out during those times. She was happy to help and support where she could, but any and all assistance would be provided only after 1pm.

But telling wasn't enough; she also had to show that she meant it. So every time someone asked Alicia for assistance during her writing hours, she explained that she wasn't available. It was uncomfortable and even a bit scary for her to do that, but she did it. She supported her words with actions, and both told and showed her family that she was serious. And within a couple of weeks, everyone had settled into the new normal and Alicia was able to get her writing done – and to meet a whole host of her own needs as a result.

USE THE 5 Cs TO ADDRESS YOUR OWN OTHERS-CENTREDNESS

Identify a goal or desire that your others-centredness is getting in the way of your achieving.

1. *Get clear* on what's going on. Step away from the situation and look at it objectively so you get a clear picture of all the competing demands and difficulties.
2. Remember that you have *choice* in everything you do — from if you do things, to how you do them. Do you choose to do it? Will doing it make you happy, add value to your life, have a positive outcome? If you do choose to do it, what is the best way for it to get done?
3. Make a *commitment* to yourself and, if necessary, contract with others, and stick to it.
4. You need to get clear in your mind and, if appropriate, the other person's mind, about what the *consequences* will be, both good and bad, of sticking or not sticking to the commitment.
5. How are you going to *communicate* your chosen path to others? Are you going to tell them, show them, or both?

WHAT'S YOUR SUPERPOWER?

As motivational speaker and business consultant Marcus Buckingham points out in his book *Find Your Strongest Life,* we all have unique strengths that are a combination of all of our life experiences and learning, as well as our innate skills, which are those things that we were born with an ability to do well.

When we allow ourselves to pay attention to what we're *good* at, we get even better at it. When we allow ourselves to learn more, grow more and experience more, we strengthen our strengths.

A superpower is the expression of all those symbiotic strengths and experiences. For example, my superpower is reading: books, moods, people, atmosphere, undercurrents, feelings, emotions, themes, trends – you name it, I can read it, mostly without even trying.

WHAT ABOUT YOU?

What is your superpower?

How are you showcasing your superpower?

Are you able to grow it and make the most of it?

If your superpower isn't getting the attention it deserves, how can you remedy that?

At work or at home, how can you pay attention to your strengths and make them even stronger?

7

Your interactions

Miscommunication and feeling misunderstood are sources of enormous conflict and unhappiness in our lives and contribute to feelings of being overwhelmed and burned out. The way we feel when we're communicating also often plays a role in our exhaustion.

Psychiatrist Eric Berne, the so-called 'father' of Transactional Analysis and the author of *Games People Play*, was interested in understanding interpersonal interactions (or transactions, as he called them). He believed that only a very small fraction of our communication is words-based. It isn't so much the words that are being used as the way we're feeling when we're using the words that determines how our message is received and responded to.

The ego states

Berne theorised that we all communicate from three ego states: Parent, Adult and Child. Simplified, when we're in our Parent ego state, we're nurturing *or* critical/controlling; in our Adult ego state we're calm, rational and empowered; and in our Child ego state, we're carefree and untroubled *or* we're scared, *or* we're sulky and aggressive. (I've simplified Berne's descriptions slightly to make it a bit easier for my clients to recognise their own ego state thoughts and feelings.)

THE PARENT EGO STATE
Our 'Nurturing Parent' causes us to be very kind, very loving, very maternal; it's the ego state we're in when we're feeling compelled to help the people around us or look after them or make things better for them. By contrast, the 'Critical and Controlling Parent' part of us is disapproving, judgemental and unsympathetic; it's the part that makes us point our finger and say things like 'How could you…?' and 'You should have…' and 'Why can't you…?'. Both Parent ego states use up a lot of energy – heated and bossy energy on the part of Critical Parent, and solicitous energy from the Nurturing Parent.

THE ADULT EGO STATE
When we're in our Adult ego state we respond thoughtfully and constructively rather than reacting emotionally and inappropriately to what's going on around us. We're the best and most effective versions of ourselves, and our energy expenditure is minimal.

THE CHILD EGO STATE
The Child ego state has three guises. We're in Natural or Free Child when we allow ourselves to play and laugh and have fun; the Natural Child comes out to play when we're hanging out with our own children or spending time with good friends who we feel safe to be silly with. The Frightened Child is the part of us that's very scared of being hurt, rejected or shamed. When you get a message from your love interest that says, 'We need to talk,' the Frightened Child in you causes your palms to begin to sweat in fear of a possible breakup; when you're walking towards your boss's office with shaky legs and a pounding heart, or when you feel so scared of messing up a presentation that you think you may vomit, that's your Frightened Child talking. The Rebellious Child is the part of us that

won't be bullied, won't be told what to do, won't toe the line just to keep the peace. It's the part of us that folds our arms, stamps our foot and, with a stuck-out lower lip, proclaims (either silently or out loud), 'You're not the boss of me!'

Our Rebellious Child requires an enormous amount of energy, as does our Frightened Child. Interestingly, our Natural Child is the ego state that actually generates energy, and it's the one we're least likely to find ourselves in.

UNDERSTANDING HOW THE EGO STATES COMMUNICATE
The ego states are usually visually represented as three circles, one above another, like a set of traffic lights, with Parent on top, Adult in the middle and Child at the bottom. This visual is crucial because one of the most important aspects of Transactional Analysis is the understanding that transactions between people take place in straight lines.

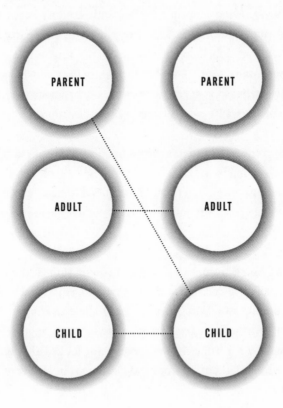

The person who initiates the transaction (or communication) stimulates a response from the person being communicated with. Depending on what ego state the initiator is in when beginning the transaction, the person being communicated with will usually respond automatically and unconsciously from the ego state that's opposite, for example, a Critical/Controlling Parent will be responded to by a Frightened or Rebellious Child, and a Rebellious or Frightened Child will be met by a Controlling/Critical or Nurturing Parent.

The person who initiates the transaction sets the tone, so if you can start a communication from your Adult ego state, the person you're transacting with is more likely to respond from their Adult ego state. The transactions that take place between people are, however, greatly influenced by the background and personality of each person involved in the transaction, as well as the context of the communication.

Things get a little more heated (and exhausting) when the transactions become stuck in an ever-growing loop of stimulus and response between the Parent and Child ego states. The more Critical or Nurturing one party becomes, the more Frightened or Rebellious the other party might become which, in turn, encourages more Critical or Nurturing feelings and behaviours. These transactions are the reason we get into heated conversations that get hotter and hotter until someone walks away (or breaks the transaction).

'I know he isn't going to have remembered to do anything about supper tonight. He never does anything I ask him to. All I want to do after this hellish day is have a bath before eating a nice dinner that I haven't had to make and then go to bed. Instead, I'm going to get home and have to find something to start cooking, from scratch...'

Anna is driving home from a challenging 12-hour shift at the hospice where she works as a palliative-care nurse. She's exhausted, emotional and hungry. Her thoughts are running away with her and seem to be escalating as she gets closer to home. 'If he hasn't made supper I'm going to be really angry. I'm so sick and tired of looking after everyone else and never being looked after back. He knows Thursdays are my hardest days at work and I just won't be able to deal with it if he hasn't thought about dinner.'

By the time Anna walks through the door she's worked herself up into a rage. She's so thoroughly managed to convince herself that her husband will disappoint her that she's somewhat taken aback to find the table laid, the house smelling of roasting chicken and her husband welcoming her with a pleased-with-himself smile. Still caught up in her Critical Parent, Anna sees only the pile of potato peelings and unwashed pans. 'Why do you always have to make such a mess when you cook? Can't you clean up after yourself like a grownup? Why is it always me who has to pick up after everyone else?'

Her husband, understandably, responds to this like a sulky child: 'Fine! I'll never make supper again. Next week you can get takeaways. Nothing I do is ever good enough for you. I'm not hungry any more; I'm going out to watch the soccer.'

In a couple of minutes, Anna has managed to alienate her husband, make herself feel even more stressed and sad, and ruin their evening. Her Critical Parent was determined to find something to be disappointed by – and she found it. And her husband responded defensively from his Rebellious Child ego state.

As we can see with Anna, the more overwhelmed, tired and burned out we are, the more out of control we feel and the more we try to control what's going on around us. Our Parent ego states come on strong and elicit the Child ego states in the people around us. And that just makes us feel more tired and stressed and overwhelmed and burned out.

UNDERSTANDING WHERE OUR RESPONSES COME FROM

Andrew was the chief executive of a company that had expanded very rapidly and was predominantly staffed by young professionals in their first jobs. Andrew tried very hard to not take on a paternal role and was very conscious of how he communicated with his staff. He came for coaching with me because he was irritable and exhausted at work, and feared for workplace harmony if he didn't do something to change the dynamic. He was fed up with running around and picking up after his employees, fixing what they weren't able or willing to do well enough themselves.

'I've explained to them the consequences of not getting the job done right, I've told them that they must ask for help if there's something they don't understand,

I've offered them my help, and they don't take it. Instead, they pretend to know what they're doing, and they keep messing up. I'm going to start losing clients and they're going to start losing their jobs if they don't up their game. And I really don't want them to lose their jobs. It would be a terrible blow to their confidence and, with the economy being what it is, they may not find other work, which will mean they and their families will be in deep trouble.'

As I listened to Andrew, I was struck by the lack of congruence between what he was saying and how he was feeling. On the face of it, his words were extremely rational and appropriate – very Adult. But the way he was feeling when he said them wasn't Adult at all; he was switching from Nurturing Parent to Critical Parent and back to Nurturing Parent, all in the space of a few seconds.

There are two aspects of Berne's theory that I always impress on my clients. The first is that our responses to the initiator's stimuli are *automatic and unconscious*, and the second is that we're responding not to the words we hear, but to *the way the person is feeling* when they use those words – i.e., to the ego state they're in. Unless we mindfully pay a lot of attention to the transactions we're engaging in, and consciously choose the ego states from which we communicate, we'll get into automatic and reactive interactions that are unconscious and often unhelpful.

When I asked Andrew how he was feeling when he said the words, he thought about it for a bit and then started to laugh. He raised his head from where he'd been resting it in his hands and sat up straighter, and I could see him moving into his Adult ego state. He was able to see that the more parental he felt, the more childlike his staff became. And the more they were in their Child ego states, the more he was in his Parent ego states.

Happily, Andrew was able to switch from Parent into Adult and very soon his staff stepped up into their Adult states as well. Almost all of his concerns were dealt with and dispatched. Andrew's stress levels decreased as his employees started taking more responsibility, which in turn encouraged his staff to take more ownership of the business and their work.

Optimal communication takes place when both people involved in the transaction are in their Adult ego states, but it's very easy for a Child or Parent

ego state to be triggered in transactions that are uncomfortable for either
When I'm describing Transactional Analysis to my clients, I explain that we learn
how to be in the world by watching the grownups. I ask them to think about the
people who took care of them when they were children and to try to identify and
describe the nature of the transactions that they witnessed between their parents
(or caregivers) – particularly at times of stress.

I've had this conversation with hundreds of people and can count on one hand
those who've described seeing Adult-to-Adult transactions at home. I'm not sure
if this is a global phenomenon but I do know that for those of us living in South
Africa, Adult-to-Adult communication and transactions aren't a familiar sight.
For as far back as anyone can remember, our country has erred on the side of a
Parent–Child model of communication. For centuries, there's been a minority
of people exerting power over the majority: a finger-waving Controlling Parent
telling Frightened and/or Rebellious Children what to think, what to do, how to
do it, who not to do it with, where to go, where not to go…

The vast majority of South Africans have never witnessed, let alone experienced,
Adult-to-Adult communication, especially under stressed circumstances. So
we don't know how to have them ourselves. It's no wonder that so often we get
sucked into exhausting, stressful and unproductive communication transactions.

It's very easy to slip into Parent or Child in our communications, particularly
when we're tired, anxious or stressed. To compound matters, the more tired and
burned out we are, the harder it is to move into and stay in Adult. But if we are to
reach a state of neutral calm, we need to consciously communicate and transact
from our Adult ego state as often as possible.

ADULTING

It's always good to have someone we can look up to, to strive to be like. Choosing a role model allows us to construct a set of goalposts — something to aim for. Picking someone who we'd like to be like helps us to identify the qualities and traits that we'd like to foster in ourselves.

For example, I — like so many others I know — regard Nelson Mandela as a good role model. Some of the things about him that I try to emulate are:

* His integrity
* His generosity and kindness
* His wisdom
* His patience
* His ability to forgive
* His intelligence — both emotional and intellectual
* His sense of humour
* His ability to see the big picture
* His ability to bring people together
* His discipline

I know I won't ever reach his levels of achievement in every area, but if I try very hard, I can maybe come close to getting at least some of them right.

Who do you admire?
What about them inspires you?
How can you be more like that person now?

How do you imagine they would respond to and manage any situation or transaction that you've found difficult or fear you'll find difficult? Imagining how your role model would feel and behave will help you to get into your own Adult ego state.

FIND SOMETHING TO CELEBRATE

When the world generally and your world in particular feels treacherous and out of control, it helps to pay active attention to noticing and appreciating what's right in it.

It doesn't always feel like it, but good things do happen – more often than we think. A smile from a stranger, recognition for a job well done, a beautiful flower, hearing about a good Samaritan, connecting with a colleague – there's a lot of good out there.

And the more good things we look for, the more good things we see.

The Drama Triangle

You know that friend or relative who always seems to be having a crisis? The one who sounds so needy and helpless that you invariably drop whatever you're doing to talk to her (or him) and try to make her feel better? The one who needs you so often that sometimes you lose your temper and shout that you wish she'd just get her life together and stop expecting you to pick up the pieces? And then you feel so bad for losing it that you overcompensate and listen to her woes late into the night?

We all have relationships in which we struggle to remain our calm, rational, Adult selves. And when we slip out of our Adult ego state, it's very hard to resist being sucked into the horrible, stressful and disheartening Victim-Rescuer-Persecutor dynamic of the Drama Triangle.

The Karpman Drama Triangle is a Transactional-Analysis model that I frequently use to help my clients understand why and how we all get into unhealthy patterns in our relationships. A student of Eric Berne's, Stephen Karpman developed the Drama Triangle to throw some light on why people get into and stay in dysfunctional and codependent relationships. (The Karpman Drama Triangle is often used to support people undergoing addiction support as well as those undergoing support for living with people with addictions. The discussion of the Drama Triangle in this book is for a different and less complex context than that of the addiction and codependence realms.)

I think the Drama Triangle is equally helpful in explaining why and how we all shift from feeling needy and demanding one minute, to loving and nurturing and responsible the next, and then just as suddenly to angry and punitive. It provides a kind and compassionate understanding of why it's so easy to get into destructive, ongoing and exhausting interactions, not just with the people we're closest to but with everyone we encounter.

We can get sucked into the Drama Triangle at work, at home, with our friends and family... basically, wherever we're in a relationship or interaction of any kind. We all fall into the Drama Triangle in different areas of our lives and play this drama out regularly and frequently.

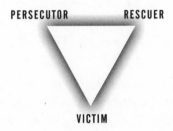

PERSECUTOR   RESCUER

VICTIM

In this upside-down triangle, the Victim is at the bottom, the Persecutor (what I call the bully) is at the top left, and the Rescuer is at the top right.

Few people *choose* to be the bully or the Victim or the Rescuer; the roles are usually filled unconsciously, and the power dynamics are played out unconsciously. We become the bully or Persecutor when we're in our Critical/Controlling Parent ego state. When we're in our Nurturing Parent ego state, we're more likely to be the Rescuer, and when we're in our Child ego state, we feel and act like the Victim.

The roles we occupy aren't static. We shift from one to the other quickly and effortlessly. This is why you can go from feeling sorry for your needy friend, to wanting to shake some sense into her, to feeling sorry for yourself when she responds to your anger with her own anger, and then back to wanting to fix everything for her – all within a few moments.

And we can be in multiple triangles simultaneously, playing different roles in different areas of our lives. We could be feeling like a Victim of our bullying boss at work, while we're playing Rescuer to our needy friend, also while Persecuting our partner for forgetting our anniversary – all at the same time. Take Anna, the hospice nurse, who spends a lot of time in the Rescuer role at work, but when she gets home, she's so stressed by the responsibility of looking after everyone in her professional life that she's quick to feel like a Victim and/or Persecutor. And, because all of it happens unconsciously, it's very confusing and exhausting.

THE RESCUER ROLE AND BURNOUT

The Rescuer role in relationships is the one that leaves us particularly vulnerable to burnout. This is the role that propels us to do things that we don't want to do, to be all things to all people, and to look after others at our own emotional and energy expense. It's the position that breeds resentment and anger that, unexpressed, will manifest in illness, exhaustion and/or depression and burnout. And, as we know, our Survivor Self frequently feels compelled to play the Rescuer. We 'rescue' others when we don't trust that they're able to look after themselves (or us).

Imraan spent a great deal of time at work because it was only after everyone else had left to go home in the afternoon that he could turn his attention to his own work. All day he answered questions, gave advice, showed others how to do their tasks and sometimes (okay, often) actually did tasks for his colleagues. All of his colleagues and subordinates knew that, if they looked needy enough, Imraan would step in and help them. He couldn't bear to sit back and watch somebody struggle, and his staff would take full advantage of his nurturing, rescuing nature. He knew he should've been helping his staff to learn how to do the tasks themselves, but he was so busy and stressed and stretched that it was easier and quicker for him to do it for them.

Every now and then, when his own to-do list pushed his stress levels sky-high, he'd lose it completely and shout about how incompetent they all were, threaten demotions or dismissals, and then feel so bad about being a monster that he'd apologise and carry on doing everyone else's work and neglecting his own.

Imraan had created a rather wicked problem for himself: not only was he adding enormously to his own workload, his 'helping' his colleagues was also serving only to make them more dependent on him, and less competent, less confident and less motivated to carry out their own responsibilities.

WHEN YOU RESCUE EVERYONE ELSE, YOU MAKE A VICTIM OF YOURSELF

This is one of my truest and most powerful life lessons – and one of the most difficult to learn.

Over and over again I find myself doing something to rescue someone and regretting it. What starts with my feeling sorry for someone else ends up with my feeling very sorry for myself. So many incidents spring to mind, usually involving my bending over backwards to accommodate someone who then lets me down, or saying yes instead of no because I don't want to hurt anyone's feelings (other than my own, of course).

And it's not just me. My clients fall into this trap too. You probably do too.

So how do we learn the lesson? There are three things we can do to stop making this mistake.

1. **Distinguish between helping and rescuing.** Helping is a conscious contract between the helper and the person being helped. It implies some degree of cooperation and agreement, with one person wanting or needing the help that the other person is able and willing to give. Rescuing, however, implies a more one-sided effort by one (powerful) person to save another (powerless) person. Unless you're a firefighter, paramedic or lifeguard, it's not your business or responsibility to rescue others.

2. **Mind your own business.** So often we rush in – uninvited – where angels fear to tread. We see something that brings out our inner saviour and we want to run to the rescue, even if we haven't been asked to. We put our own agenda at risk by trying to fix someone else's problem. Or we waste our own time and energy trying to change something that isn't ours to change.

3. **Make a mindful choice.** Just because we can, doesn't mean we must. We can *choose* if and how we want to offer help or provide it when it's asked for.

We need to stay in our own lanes, mind our own business and wait to be asked.

The Drama Triangle is extremely powerful – I often say I think it should be named the Bermuda Triangle of Drama because it's so difficult to resist being sucked into, and once you're in it, it's equally difficult to get out of. But it's possible to both leave and stay out of the drama. It requires being mindful and vigilant about how we behave in our interactions with others and within ourselves. Once we understand the dynamics and are able to choose how we respond to people and situations, we can drop the drama and find peace and calm.

As we know, the Drama Triangle is depicted as an upside-down triangle illustrating the three ego states of Critical/Controlling Parent, Nurturing Parent, and Child. You'll have noticed that there's no Adult in the Drama Triangle. That's because it's not possible to be in the Drama Triangle in our Adult ego state. If we're able to move into our Adult ego state, we're able to either move out of the drama, or avoid getting into it in the first place.

We can also stay out of the Drama Triangle by staying in our own business. Byron Katie says that there are three kinds of 'business': my business, your business and God's business.

When we're in God's business, we're concerning ourselves with things over which no one has control – the plane crashing, when the drought is going to break, the world coming to an end… When we're in God's business, we're spending (or wasting) our energy on thoughts and anxieties that are going to go nowhere fast.

When we're in someone else's business, we're concerning ourselves with things that don't belong to us, and over which we also have no control. We worry about what they think and feel, the choices they may or may not make, and how they may or may not behave. We think about what they need, what they want and what they like – often at the expense of our own needs, wants and likes. We may even tell them what they should be wanting, thinking or feeling, or how they should be behaving – even if they haven't asked. When we're in other people's business, we're in our Parent (either Critical or Nurturing) ego state, and it's often when we take on the bully or Rescuer role.

When we let other people into our business, we allow them to tell us what we should be thinking, feeling, wanting or liking. We weaken our own boundaries and open ourselves up to being discounted, overlooked, bullied or rescued. We allow ourselves to feel weak and childlike – we're in the Child ego state and/or the Victim role.

When we're in our own business, taking responsibility for our own thoughts, feelings and actions, and not expecting others to take responsibility for us, or to need us to take responsibility for them, we're in our Adult ego state and out of the Drama Triangle.

Staying in our own business, and keeping others out of it, can be hard because from an early age many of us have been dragged into other people's business and/or have had other people encroaching on ours. It's sometimes hard to know where we end and where our business ends, and where someone else and their business begins.

The week after we worked on the Drama Triangle and understood how Imraan was being sucked into it at work, he came into my office with new spring in his step. 'I'm managing to get out and stay out of the Drama Triangle!' he said. 'I used the 5 Cs to help me get clear on what was going on, and to decide how I was going to leave the drama. I realised that it *is* my business to help my staff to do their work, but it *isn't* my business to do their work for them.

'I thought through how I was going to respond to requests for assistance and made a commitment to myself about how to manage my staff moving forward. The very next day, one of my staff members came to me to ask for help; she said she couldn't do something that was urgent and due that afternoon. Before, I would've just done the task for her, but this time I summoned up Barack Obama [Imraan's adult role model], sat with her for 30 minutes and helped her think through what she needed to do – and then I sent her away to do it. She came back a couple of hours later to show me what she'd done and it was great. It was a revelation for both of us!'

By getting into his Adult ego state and taking responsibility for only his own business, Imraan enabled his staff to step up and into their roles (and business).

And he was able to finish his own work during working hours, and start doing things after work that fed his body, mind and soul.

Anna also happily left the Drama Triangle. Referring to her Adult role model (the mother of a friend), she was able to use the 5 Cs to rein in her anger when her husband didn't immediately tidy up after himself in the kitchen, and she was also able to express her appreciation for his care and to allow herself to enjoy the dinners he made for her, before helping him to tidy the kitchen and stack the dishwasher before bed.

YOUR TURN TO DROP THE DRAMA

Think of the Drama Triangles you're in currently or have been in in the past. You'll probably find that there are a few. Taking them one at a time, identify:

❋ The roles you play (Persecutor, Rescuer or Victim)

❋ The ego states you operate from

❋ Whose business you're in

Do you notice any patterns? Are there particular people with whom you play particular roles? Are there certain people, activities or places that seem to suck you into the drama very easily?

Now, summon up that Adult role model of yours, move into your Adult ego state, ask yourself what your business is, and step away from the drama.

The internal Drama Triangle

Stephen Karpman developed the Drama Triangle to explain the dynamics that keep people in troubled relationships or stuck in an endless loop of rescuing-bullying-feeling victimised. But I don't think that the application of the triangle is limited to interactions between two or more people. I think that the vast majority of us experience an internal Drama Triangle that sees us playing the roles of Victim, Rescuer and Persecutor towards and within ourselves. Our Critical and Nurturing Parent, and Frightened and Rebellious Child ego states often get into an argument among themselves. This is what I call the internal Drama Triangle.

Have you ever been nervous about needing to do something you don't feel comfortable doing? Maybe a presentation at work or a speech at a wedding? The night before the event, you may have experienced a thought process that looked a little like this:

'What if I make a fool of myself and everyone laughs at me or feels sorry for me or thinks I'm stupid?'

'I won't make a fool of myself. I've prepared well and I'm going to be dressed for success in my lucky shirt that always makes me feel brave and competent and it'll be fine. If it gets too scary, I'll just imagine them all naked.'

'What happens if my shirt buttons pop open in the middle of my talk and everyone laughs at me?'

'Well, if I hadn't spent my whole life overeating that wouldn't be a problem. I'm too fat. I'm too stupid and I'm not good enough to do this properly.'

'I'm never going to get what I want because I always mess things up. Like the time that I forgot to/didn't...'

When we get trapped in our minds, remembering bad things that have happened (and often remembering them as worse than they really were) or imagining bad things that may happen, we get trapped in an internal Drama Triangle of horror, despair and anxiety. We go around and around in mental circles of bullying, then trying to rescue ourselves from imagined hardships and horrors. It's exhausting and anxiety-provoking and, I believe, is a leading contributor to burnout.

The internal Drama Triangle doesn't only manifest in repetitive and anxiety-provoking thoughts, it often translates into repetitive and destructive actions too.

Kati used to come home from a hard day at work feeling exhausted and strung out. Because of her burnout, she was using up all the precious energy she could muster trying to be effective at work. The relief she felt to be back in her sanctuary was soon replaced by worry, and the scary thoughts would start to race: 'The session with the boss didn't go very well, maybe he thinks I'm not up for the job! How can I have been so stupid in our meeting? Why was I so inarticulate…?'

Within a few minutes of walking through the front door, Kati would've convinced herself that her job was in danger and it was all her own fault; she was a walking disaster – always had been, always would be.

She turned to chocolate, one of the drugs of choice for people with burnout. It made her feel better while she was chewing and swallowing, but when it was finished, she'd feel awful – worse than before. Then, her internal dialogue would become even more colourful: 'You're so weak. No wonder you're about to be fired – you're such a pig. You're pathetic.'

Round and round these thoughts would go, helping Kati descend into a downward spiral of bullying herself, trying to make herself feel better, and then bullying herself some more. The more she criticised herself, the worse she'd feel, and the worse she felt, the more chocolate she had to eat… and so it went on.

I see this cycle of self-defeat a lot in my coaching room, and it doesn't have to be related to food, although that's a common stick with which clients beat themselves. I believe that the internal Drama Triangle is to blame for many of the compulsive habits we punish ourselves for falling prey to. We feel sorry for ourselves for whatever reason, so we rescue ourselves by self-soothing with our drug of choice (food, alcohol, cigarettes, reading, procrastinating, binge-watching TV), only to persecute ourselves for being so weak, which makes us feel weaker, so we need to rescue ourselves… and so it continues.

It's not just the actions we take that wear us out, it's also the actions we don't take – the thoughts that we allow to keep circling like vultures, waiting for an opportunity to pick us apart.

It's a nasty cycle to be stuck in, and when we have burnout we have so little energy that it's almost impossible to resist the drama (both internal and external) or leave it when we find ourselves there. But it is possible, and not that difficult, to break it. Once you have a clearer idea of what your personal self-defeat cycle looks like, you can start to stop it. Awareness is the most important prerequisite for change. Knowing what you're doing, and when you're doing it, will allow you to change.

The 5 Cs helped Kati to realise that she was always much harder on herself when she was tired and hungry; she worked out that her inner voice was much more bullying and critical when she hadn't eaten. Once she became aware of what was going on in her internal Drama Triangle, she made a commitment to herself to eat more regularly and thus stop the negative self-talk before it started. To help herself enforce this, she took healthy snacks and food to work, and set her phone to remind herself to eat something every three hours.

Kati also contracted with herself that, when she did need comforting, she'd turn to things that genuinely made her feel better – a hot shower, talking to her husband, and going to yoga with a friend were some of the alternatives to chocolate that she identified for herself. She also gave herself permission to eat some chocolate – as long as she'd eaten a healthy meal beforehand.

Lastly, she made a commitment to herself to leave work behind when she walked through her front door, and consciously stopped herself from worrying about work during non-working hours.

Through being mindful and aware, Kati was able to change her internal dialogue from a bullying and self-defeating one into a constructive and self-supporting one.

FROM SELF-DEFEAT TO SELF-RELEASE IN 3 EASY STEPS

Step 1.

Be aware of the internal Drama Triangle-induced cycle of self-defeat. Where do you notice cycles of self-defeat in your own life? For example, 'Whenever I feel that I have to do something, I procrastinate.' What's your preferred method of self-rescue? For example, 'Reading – mostly novels, but anything will do.'

Step 2.

Step into your Adult ego state and identify what constructive actions you can take in order to break your cycle of self-defeat. For example, when I'm in my Nelson Mandela-inspired Adult ego state, I can see that my procrastination is nothing more than my Rebellious Child telling my Critical Parent, 'You're not the boss of me!' My Adult ego state can assess, calmly and rationally, if the task I've been avoiding is really necessary for me to do. Then I can apply the 'if or how' tool; for example, I can ask for help to do my tax returns, I can have some nice music playing in the background when I'm doing tasks that don't require too much mental effort, or I can do boring work in a coffee shop where I won't feel so lonely and resentful about it.

Step 3.

Make a contract with your Adult ego state that will help you to break the cycle and keep it broken. The 5 Cs tool will help you to do this.

DO SOMETHING DIFFERENT

It isn't just our moods and our relationships that can get into a rut – our minds can too. When we do the same things the same ways over and over again, our brains shift into autopilot and stop working as well as they should. We keep our brains and our relationships healthy when we challenge them by doing things differently every now and then.

Change your office around, change your chair, take a different route to the bathroom/kitchen, use a different mug for your tea, get a new pen. It doesn't matter what change you make – big or small, any change is enough to challenge your brain to do some exercise.

8

Anxiety and burnout

This chapter is intended to show how anxiety affects and is affected by burnout, and doesn't in any way aim to serve as an alternative to working with a trained professional. Anxiety and panic attacks are serious conditions that need the attention of a medical or mental-health professional. If you're experiencing anxiety and/or panic, please don't delay in seeking help.

Just as we suffer from cumulative burnout, we also experience stress and anxiety on many interrelated levels. There are all manner of things in our inner world that lead to or exacerbate anxiety. Life in the modern world is very emotionally demanding: we're under pressure to perform at work, at home, in our relationships, in our studies. We're expected to look good, feel good and do good all the time.

Then there's the outer world, which adds another, bigger and scarier layer to our feelings of insecurity and being out-of-control. Fear of change, political instability, crime and violence, exposure to the horrors that are gripping the world in general and our own country in particular (yes, we're affected by what we're exposed to in the media). All of this leads to what I call 'absorbed anxiety'. And absorbed anxiety is perhaps the most difficult kind of anxiety to deal with because it's not ours to address.

Some of the people I've worked with who suffer the most complex and hard-to-shift burnout have been journalists, doctors and teachers who are exposed to the anxiety, stress, fear and even trauma of every one of the many people they come into contact with every day.

It's not just that the news arena is a high-stress, deadline-driven environment; the people who work in news are also constantly seeing, speaking, reading, writing and hearing about distressing events. Having to report on horrors that they have no power to influence is exhausting, overwhelming and a fast track to burnout. Teachers, similarly, work in a high-stress, deadline-driven environment and are tasked with developing and supporting students who may be experiencing a range of emotional, material and physical hardships that they bring to school with them. It isn't possible for a committed and empathetic teacher to remain untouched by the struggles of their students. The inability to make a meaningful change in the life circumstances of the young people they inevitably build bonds with is very worrying and wearying. So, too, is the inability to change the life circumstances that are often major contributors to the diseases that doctors and nurses must treat in their patients.

We're mostly helpless in making things better globally or even locally, so we need to learn how to make things better for ourselves. We need to do what we can, wherever and whenever we can, to make our inner and outer worlds feel as predictable and contained (and containing) as possible. We need to manage stress and anxiety if we're to reduce burnout.

In moderation, stress can be a positive thing in our lives. Positive stress stimulates us to push ourselves to achieve goals that may otherwise be unattainable – like passing exams, learning to drive or finishing that promotion-dependent presentation. But negative stress (or even too much positive stress) eats away at our wellbeing by making us feel anxious and out of control. Over time, stress erodes our resilience and can lead to anxiety and burnout. The more burned out we are, the more affected we are by anxiety and stress. The more anxious and stressed we feel, the more prone we are to burning out.

The anxiety triangle

Commonly, anxiety is understood to be a feeling of worry, nervousness or unease, typically about an imminent event or something with an uncertain outcome. My own description of anxiety is a feeling of worry, nervousness or unease, typically about a *real or imagined* imminent event or something with an uncertain *real or imagined* outcome.

When we get trapped in our internal Drama Triangle – or what I like to call the anxiety triangle – we often overlook reality in favour of imagined outcomes, and this contributes enormously to our stress and anxiety, to our mental, emotional and physical detriment.

When we feel anxious, we experience a surge in adrenaline and, in the absence of an actual physical foe to fight or from which to flee, we become frozen in fear-laden flights of horrible fearful fantasy. A mild concern about a button popping off a shirt in the middle of a big presentation quickly escalates and, before you know it, you're unemployed and homeless, starving and lonely, enduring the devastation of climate change-induced drought, floods and general apocalypse, trying to survive on the streets of the war-ravaged country your homeland is surely about to become, wondering how you're going to endure the nuclear winter that will result from the imminent pressing of the big red button by someone up north.

When we're hanging out in the anxiety triangle, we become drenched in adrenaline – pickled, marinated in adrenaline. When we scare ourselves by imagining all sorts of unspeakable horrors, our bodies release a cocktail of adrenaline and cortisol – the so-called 'stress hormones' that propel our bodies into fight or flight. Like a runaway freight train, our anxiety starts off slowly but quickly gains speed until it crashes through the rails and sinks in a sea of imagined horrors.

The problem is that our bodies can't tell the difference between real and imagined fears. As soon as we think about something that makes us fearful, our bodies release the stress hormones that help us to protect ourselves. Our heart beats faster, our breathing gets quicker, we start to perspire, and we feel shaky and edgy. If we don't do anything to release the stress hormones, they circulate in our body, making us feel more and more anxious, more and more fearful, and more and more trapped inside ourselves. If the anxiety and stress-hormone cocktail is too strong, we may experience a panic attack – an experience so terrifying and debilitating that it's often mistaken for a heart attack.

Mpho came to see me because he'd been having panic attacks at work. He'd always loved his work and was very good at it but one day, seemingly out of the blue, he felt as though he was about to have a heart attack during the weekly management meeting. For no apparent reason, his heart started beating quickly, his breathing became shallow and fast, sweat began pouring down his face and back, and he thought he was going to pass out. He was convinced that his time had come.

Luckily, someone in the meeting recognised what was happening and, instead of calling an ambulance, got Mpho to calm down and feel better by talking him through it and helping him to focus on his breathing. He was booked off work for a couple of months and came to me for coaching to help him make sense of what had happened.

He told me that he'd been working 12-hour days six days a week for the four years he'd been in this job. Although he loved his work and found it exciting and stimulating (mostly positively so), he and his wife had recently had a baby and he was feeling torn between working at his usual pace, spending time with his wife and daughter, and finding time to see friends and do some exercise.

It was a pretty textbook case of burnout – but why the panic attacks? There was no doubt that he'd been ignoring and pushing through his symptoms of burnout for quite a while, which certainly contributed to the episodes of overwhelming anxiety (the more we ignore our bodies, the louder they need to scream to be heard) but I felt that there was something deeper going on with Mpho.

Through more conversation it emerged that he was the eldest child and only son of a single mother. His father had left the family when Mpho was 5 and his sister was 2. For a couple of years, his dad was peripherally involved with the family, but his involvement was unpredictable and inconsistent at best and irresponsibly unreliable at worst. Mpho soon came to realise that his father's unreliability was having a very serious and detrimental impact on his mother, who suffered from anxiety and depression for much of Mpho's childhood.

Mpho's Survivor Self stepped in and turned him into the most reliable, responsible and responsive little boy he could be. 'You can rely on me!' became Mpho's unconscious vision and mission. At home, at school, at work and beyond – Mpho's defining strength was his reliability.

This made him an excellent and hardworking employee, and a prime candidate for burnout. It also made him susceptible to anxiety and panic when he reached the point of feeling that he couldn't be relied on any longer. He literally started to panic in that meeting when he suddenly felt too tired to carry on being hardworking and reliable SuperMpho.

The thing about our Survivor Self is that, although it really does help us to survive, it can also drive us to collapse. As soon as we feel any of the emotional or physical discomfort that comes with burnout and anxiety, our Survivor Self is triggered. Without our being aware of it, our Survivor Self often pushes us to do more, be more, achieve more as a way to protect us from possible danger. Unfortunately, our Survivor Self can be a hard taskmaster and frequently exacerbates and escalates the anxiety, stress and burnout.

Mpho and I had a conversation about how he thought his Survivor Self may have been leading him astray. He admitted that his war cry, 'You can rely on me!' had started to make him feel panicky and trapped, as if he had no choice. 'I have to be the one everyone relies on all the time, for everything, even things I don't want to do,' he said. I pointed out that he's now an adult and that he does have a choice, and he realised that he wanted to continue to be reliable, because it was important to him, but he wanted to be reliable in those things that he'd chosen to take on, rather than those that he felt he had to take on. He also wanted to rely on himself to make the right choices about what he should be saying yes to and what he could say no to.

As awful and terrifying and lethal as panic attacks can feel, with the right support in making sense of them, they can be a valuable source of information for us. Similarly, when we're able to recognise the beliefs that our Survivor Self continues to hold on to, we're able to update them and turn them into beliefs that will carry on serving us into adulthood and beyond.

BREATHE

Stop what you're doing and pay attention to your breathing. Are you taking deep, slow breaths? Or are you panting like a dog on a hot day?

Because breathing is as natural as, well, breathing, we tend not to pay too much attention to it. It's just something that happens in the background while we get on with our days (and nights). But the way we breathe has a profound impact on the way we feel, both physically and emotionally.

When we're stressed, anxious or scared we tend to take short, shallow breaths that don't fill our lungs with enough oxygen, making us more anxious, scared and stressed. It becomes a vicious cycle of stress.

The good news is that you can break that cycle by breathing properly, and it only takes a minute to fix.

* Sit comfortably.
* Breathe in for a slow count of 3, making sure it's a deep breath that reaches right down into your lungs.
* Hold in that breath for a slow count of 3.
* Breathe out for a slow count of 3, trying to empty your lungs of as much air as you can.
* Wait for a count of 3.
* Repeat 3 times (or as many times as you need to feel calmer and stronger).

Pay attention to your breathing regularly in your day. The more you practise, the better you will get at it.

Act to address anxiety

Two things are of the essence in diverting anxiety:

❋ Identifying the action you can take,

❋ Quickly.

Anxiety makes us dwell on (or obsess over, depending on your viewpoint) a lot of things that aren't only often improbable, but are also usually absolutely and completely out of our control. There's no way your insomniac worrying is going to stop a power-crazed 'leader' from starting a nuclear war. You have little enough chance of directing the behaviour of the people close to you; there's no way that a megalomaniac in another time zone is going to be swayed by your concerns. As powerful as you are, you just aren't able to change – or even influence – the actions of people with whom you have no contact.

What you *can* do, however, is get off that train of anxiety before it leaves the station. Deal with the idea of your shirt popping open, for example, as soon as it comes into your mind. What would Oprah (or whoever your Adult role model is) do? I imagine she'd wear another outfit or a different shirt – one that was a little roomier and had no history of button-popping.

Put your energy and attention into taking action where and when you can. And the sooner you can intervene in your thoughts, the better. By taking action, even if it's just mental action to start with, you can get off that train before it gathers speed and runs away with you, you can stay out of the anxiety triangle, and you can ensure that you'll be better prepared and more confident.

Also, acceptance about the things you can't change is much easier when you're taking mindful and empowering steps to change the things that you can change.

ACCEPT THE THINGS YOU CAN'T CHANGE
One of our biggest struggles is accepting that there are some things – some people, some events, some disappointments – that we can't influence or change. As hard as our Survivor Self may try, and as much as it may worry, there's nothing we can do.

All that happens when we try to change what isn't ours to change is that we exhaust ourselves both physically and emotionally. We get more disappointed and more disillusioned, more frustrated and more frayed. It doesn't get us anywhere useful or good, but increases our stress and anxiety, which contribute to burnout.

We need to find the serenity to accept that there are some things that we just can't change. When I talk about acceptance, I don't mean that you necessarily have to like or embrace it, but I do mean that you need to come to terms with the fact that there's nothing you can do to change whatever it is. Because when you accept that there are some things over which you have no influence or control – that you can't change – then you can spend your time and energy more productively on those things over which you *do* have influence or control. Like yourself: the choices you make, the paths you take, the goals you reach.

When faced with worry about something that really is beyond your control to change, it's useful to have a conversation with yourself to show yourself that whatever you're anticipating probably won't happen or that it may not be so bad if it does happen. For example, every time I find myself about to board the anxiety train to nuclear war, I summon up my inner Nelson Mandela to give me three (or more) good reasons why it may never happen – one, it hasn't happened before now, despite nuclear warheads having been around for decades; two, once the button is pressed, the game is over, and no one wants to give their toys away; and three, the people who need to push the button are far too narcissistic to contemplate killing themselves along with the rest of the population.

Through summoning up our Adult ego state, we're able to leave the anxiety triangle and talk some sense into ourselves. Try it yourself – it's really effective!

Sometimes our anxiety doesn't seem to have a clear entry point. It just descends like a cloud of amorphous greyness, threatening to pour cold water on our enjoyment of life. When that happens, I prescribe taking physical action to break the cycle. Moving your body helps to dilute the marinade of stress hormones, so go for a walk with a friend, go to gym or do some yoga, dance to your favourite song, make a meal or bake a cake, do some mindful breathing or paint your toenails...

WHAT ARE YOU GOING TO DO?

We've already had a look at deciding *if* we should engage; and, if so, *how*. Now, in addressing your anxiety, you need to assess if you *can* do something about whatever is troubling you (in other words, if it's within your realm of influence and control); and, if so, *what*.

Think about something that's been or is making you anxious right now. Ask yourself:

❋ Is there any aspect or part of it (or all of it) that you can act on?

❋ If so, what action can you take?

❋ If not, can you identify a more productive use of your time and energy and take action on something you can change?

For example, I'm anxious that there's going to be a power outage (again) today and I'm going to be stuck in traffic and late for my meeting with my tax consultant. And if I miss the meeting then maybe my tax return won't be submitted in time and then I'll be arrested and sent to prison.

❋ I can't act on if there'll be a power outage or how much traffic there'll be. But I can make sure I leave early enough for the meeting. I can also email through all my paperwork so that, even if the traffic is as horrendous as I fear it will be, my tax consultant will be able to work on the figures in my absence.

FEEL THE SUN ON YOUR SKIN

What with working long hours, many of us don't have lots of time outside in the sun. And as a result there's a growing problem of low vitamin-D levels – even among those of us who live in the sunny southern hemisphere. Symptoms of vitamin-D deficiency include overwhelming fatigue and tiredness, frequent illness and infections with longer recovery time, hair loss, bone thinning and weakness, and even depression.

It's crazy that we have access to the strongest, cheapest and most accessible source of vitamin D, and so few of us make use of it. Just a few minutes in the sun every day will give you enough vitamin D to boost your mood and your immunity. So go outside! Roll up your sleeves, roll down your socks and feel the sun on your skin. But not for too long – we don't want you to burn.

9
Spending your energy wisely

Burnout is a thief. It makes tasks that were previously easy and pleasurable hard and/or unpleasant. Many burnout sufferers find that they're no longer able to do what they previously loved.

One person I worked with stopped reading books in the aftermath of a prolonged period of untold stress that resulted in burnout; another, who'd previously produced *MasterChef*-worthy meals for her family every night, lost all interest in and inclination for cooking. One of the things that burnout has stolen from me is my ability to write for long stretches. I used to be able to write for hours on end, often until 3 or 4 in the morning; now I'm lucky if I can hold a thought and write for longer than 20 minutes at a time.

For many people, it can be devastating to think about what we've lost to burnout. But often, what's been lost is replaced by something found: the ability to be with ourselves and our thoughts and feelings, rather than running away from them and hiding in books or recipes. Our ability to pay attention to our inner world replaces our preoccupation with what's going on in the outer world. I think, for example, that some of the silver lining of my severely truncated writing stretches forces me to find a more balanced and gentle way to write. I'm now forced to manage my time and energy more maturely, and make sure I take small and powerful steps every day – no more burning the post-midnight oil for days on end. I'm more thoughtful and productive, my life is more balanced, and I'm much less stressed and exhausted.

Burnout has taught – and continues to teach – me to be more mindful about how I use and spend my energy. Where I used to go on wild energy-spending sprees that sent me to bed for days to recover, I now think about how I'm spending my energy, and what I'm spending it on. Now I understand that I need to respect my energy the same way I respect my money.

To my mind, burnout is the equivalent of being energetically broke. Sometimes we can dig ourselves out of the hole and, through a programme of debt restructuring, rehabilitate ourselves. And sometimes the debt is so huge that all we can do is file for insolvency and start all over again. In order to recover from burnout, we need to sit down and be very honest with ourselves about where we can make some savings. We also need to be ruthless about planning how to spend and save our energy moving forward.

Most of us give a lot of thought to how we manage our money and how we can get or stay financially solvent and healthy. We draw up weekly, monthly and annual budgets, plan our savings and put money aside for our retirement. But how many of us do any of that for our energy and our physical and emotional wealth? We tend to put much more emphasis on financial wellness – often at the expense of our physical wellness.

The need for an energy budget

Just as we know that we can't (or shouldn't) be blowing our financial budget on big-ticket items every month, we need to be mindful about how we allocate our energy budget. If we spend more than we make or bank, we'll go into overdraft; too much outflow will end in bankruptcy/burnout. But if we're able to save some energy by spending wisely, then we have reserves that we can draw on when and if we need to.

When we spend our energy wisely, we can avoid a crisis. When we rest, we allow our energy to accumulate some interest. When we're doing what we love and what feeds us, we're putting energy into a savings account. When we're doing what we don't want to do – the wrong things for us – we're wasting our energy. Like spending money on alcohol and cigarettes, our energy is being put into something that isn't only bad for us but is also offering no return on our investment.

It's important to be mindful of what activities, places and people give us energy, and which of those take energy away from us. Some are obvious (doing something you hate doing, for example) and others are a little more complex. For instance, one of the things that makes me feel weak at the knees (and not in a good way) just thinking about it, is shopping in a mall – the bright lights, the loud music, all the people… the sensory overload is too much for me. But when my niece and/ or nephew ask me to take them clothes shopping, I cheerfully oblige – because the sheer joy of spending time with those bright, shiny, funny and entertaining humans more than outweighs the horror of spending hours in department stores. You will, no doubt, have similar anomalies in your own energy income and expenditure spreadsheet.

You will have noticed, as you spend more time and attention on tuning in to your body and thinking about how to spend your energy, that there are certain people, tasks and places that give you energy and others that drain your energy. You will in all likelihood recognise that you're wasting some of your energy in Drama Triangles and on business that isn't yours. I have no doubt that you'll start to recognise some of the areas in your life that are contributing to or aggravating your burnout.

It isn't enough to recognise what's draining our energy; we also need to put a plug in that drain. We need to decide *if* and *how* we're going to carry on doing the things that exhaust us with no return on our energy investment. You can decide what to say no to, and what to ask for help with. And you can decide what to put down, so you can pick yourself up.

ENERGY REVENUE

Think about your last week, and list all the things you did, the people you saw and the places you went. Then ask yourself which of those gave you energy and which took energy from you.

* Where are you making energy?
* Where are you breaking even?
* Where are you running at a loss of energy?

Do you notice any patterns in what takes your energy and what creates energy for you? Where can you save energy? Where and how can you stop overspending?

Self-sabotage or self-rescue?

One of the things my burnout clients struggle with the most is feeling that their work (or anything else that used to feel fulfilling) has lost meaning for them. It's one of the cruelties of burnout that things that used to feel meaningful to us lose their colour and vibrancy. It doesn't matter if it's work, reading, cooking or anything else, in the absence of meaning, tasks can start to feel boring, mundane and, well, meaningless.

The truth is, though, that it's not just that burnout taints meaning; I believe that an absence of meaning contributes to burnout. Because without meaning, what we do is a drudge. Unfortunately, many of us – for many reasons – often find ourselves doing work that doesn't feel important or profound to us in any way. We're in it only for the salary. Too many of my clients who're experiencing burnout feel trapped by the salary that they need to earn in order to pay for all the things they have to do to make themselves feel better about doing what they hate. Holidays, massages, shoes, magazines, cars, expensive hobbies, alcohol, drugs (both over- and under-the-counter), cigarettes… these can all end up needing a hefty monthly salary.

A similar effect applies in relationships. Sometimes we're so invested in being loved and in love that we don't pay enough attention to assessing if the relationship is right for us or not – we overlook if the person we're so desperate to be loved by is the right person for us, or is loving us the way we deserve and yearn to be loved. We may find ourselves in the grips of others-centredness, Drama Triangles and many of the other ills that we've covered in this book.

But we can only fool ourselves for so long. Eventually we see, do or say something that reveals our intuitive wisdom and saves us from ourselves. It may not seem like a life jacket at the time, but it's designed to save us.

I often witness clients beating themselves up for getting in their own way. They get really cross with themselves for wasting an opportunity, messing up an interview or not studying hard enough for an exam. Clients who have burnout are angry with themselves for forgetting appointments, for being rude to their bosses, for sleeping rather than going to gym… 'I don't know why I keep sabotaging myself,' they wail. And every time I'm pretty sure that there's a very good reason. It may be an unexpected reason, but I'm convinced it's a good one nonetheless.

Because, to be honest, I'm not even sure that there's such a thing as self-sabotage. We're quick to judge ourselves negatively, but I truly believe that our essential self knows what's good for us and makes unconscious decisions that are in our best interests. According to Martha Beck, the essential self, or what psychologists refer to as the true self, is who we really are – if you could boil us down to our most basic essence, this is who you would find. Our true self knows what we like, what we don't like, what's good for us and what's bad for us – it wants to make and keep us happy.

I have a theory that what looks like self-sabotage is actually self-rescue.

It may seem, for example, that we're sabotaging ourselves by being unprepared for an interview when the truth is that we're actually saving ourselves from a job that we know deep down inside we'll hate. And running out of petrol on the way to a party may look like disorganisation, but perhaps it's by unconscious design to keep away from people and situations that aren't good for us. Similarly, forgetting appointments and oversleeping and missing gym are, I think, a result of the essential self intervening to help us get much-needed rest.

WHAT RESOLUTIONS HAVE YOU BEEN RESCUING YOURSELF FROM?

Every New Year's Eve most of us set some hastily identified resolutions. They usually have to do with self-improvement (go to gym, study further), self-esteem (lose weight, wear matching underwear) or self-actualisation (learn a new skill, find love). And they usually fall by the wayside a few weeks (or sometimes days) after the new year has started, only to be resurrected the following December.

Why do we keep resolving to do things that we don't achieve? And, more importantly, why don't we achieve those resolutions? We're quick to tell ourselves that we don't achieve our goals because we sabotage ourselves, but are we sure it isn't actually a brilliant case of self-rescue? I truly believe that our essential self knows what's good for us and makes unconscious decisions in our best interests a lot of the time.

So it may seem that we're sabotaging ourselves by eating those carbs, or by missing spinning classes at the crack of every dawn, when the truth might be that we're actually saving ourselves from grumpiness, deprivation, boredom and stiff thighs.

Make a list of some of the goals and objectives you've set for yourself in the past. Which ones (if any) did you not manage to achieve? Why do you think you weren't able to see them to fruition? How might you have been rescuing yourself or, put differently, what might you have been rescuing yourself from? Which ones (if any) did you manage to achieve? Why do you think you managed to follow through with them?

Of course we sabotage ourselves sometimes, but I think it looks very different to how we expect it to look. I think self-sabotage looks like working too hard, not eating properly, not getting enough sleep, wasting our energy worrying about things over which we have no control, not spending enough time on and with ourselves, being others-centred, rescuing everyone all the time, trying to force a relationship that's making us so anxious we need to medicate ourselves, and all the various other ways we try to do too much and take care of ourselves too little.

The paradox is that we judge ourselves negatively for not pushing hard enough, rather than for pushing too hard. Rather than asking ourselves why we've run out of steam, that Survivor Self of ours makes us try to do more on the little steam we have left. We sabotage ourselves by trying to do too much of the wrong things, and by judging ourselves mercilessly when we try a bit of self-rescue.

I had a client who judged himself mercilessly for getting the time of a job interview wrong and missing it. His job as a corporate trainer had pushed him so far beyond burnout that 'frazzled' doesn't even come close to describing him. He hated what he was doing, how he was doing it and who he was doing it with. When he got invited to an interview for a similar job in another company, he was able to summon up some enthusiasm and agreed to a time and date. And then he arrived on the right date but an hour late.

He was really very upset with himself for messing up the opportunity to move to a new job – but when I asked him if he really wanted the new job, he eventually started chuckling and confessed that, no, he didn't. And why would he? To replace one soul-destroying work situation with another isn't a solution and it's not progress. As is so often the case, what looked like self-sabotage was really self-rescue.

What are you rescuing yourself from?

Think about the last time you berated yourself for tripping yourself up. Was it really self-sabotage or was it self-rescue? And if, as I predict, a lot of it was self-rescue, what or who were you rescuing yourself from?

Think about the areas in your life where you're pushing yourself forward. Is all of that pushing healthy or is there some 'self-sabotage'?

Once you've managed to turn around the way you interpret your actions, you'll probably notice a correlation between how you're sabotaging yourself and what you're doing to rescue yourself – and what you're rescuing yourself from.

JUST DO IT!

What have you been avoiding? What are you procrastinating about? What are you putting off doing until you can do it perfectly?

I believe that we procrastinate because we're worried that we aren't able to do perfectly whatever it is we're avoiding doing. This paralysis serves only to make us more and more anxious about the task that we're avoiding.

Very few people are able to get everything absolutely right the very first time they do it, so put down your anxiety about not creating something perfect and allow yourself to create something that's good enough. Let yourself do whatever it is you've been avoiding doing. It doesn't have to be immediately perfect, it can and will be improved by revising or practising, and you can ask for help. After all, in the words of the late great online business coach Laurie Foley, 'done is better than perfect'.

10

Maintaining your burnout-free life

You're clever, creative, resourceful, innovative, responsive, flexible and tough. You're more resilient than you think you are. You're a survivor.

Every one of us has responded to the challenges and disappointments and losses we've experienced by making sense of them, by adjusting our expectations and behaviours, by surviving. But, as we've learned in the previous chapters, not all of our responses serve us as well as they used to. I hope that this book has helped you to examine your habits and patterns and make sense of your survival responses. I hope that you'll be better able to decide which thoughts, behaviours and responses need to be consciously adjusted to better serve your current and future needs. I hope that you'll make the necessary changes to ensure that your life and your place in it is more comfortable, more rewarding and more joyful.

I also hope that you're able to acknowledge, appreciate and celebrate just how resilient and resourceful you are now, and have always been. Your resilience is what's kept you intact your whole life, and it's what will help you to develop a deeper understanding of yourself – your beliefs, your fears, your drivers, how you respond to pressures – so that you can make real, sustainable changes to how you live your life, so that you can regain your health and vitality in order to maintain your burnout-free life.

STROKE YOUR OWN EGO

We all like to feel noticed and appreciated by others but we also need to pay attention to our own accomplishments. Take some time to feel pleased with yourself – it will energise you and give you the enthusiasm to continue on your way.

Think about:
* What you've done well today or this week or this month or this year.
* What you're proud of yourself for managing.
* What compliments you've received.
* What you think you do well.
* What the thing is about yourself that you most appreciate.

Write it all down. You could even write one or two on post-it notes and stick them somewhere you can see them whenever you're in need of a bit of a lift.

How you do anything is how you do everything

If you're anything like me (and the rest of the world), you have a few little habits that are microscopic reflections of your way of being in the world more broadly. For instance, I have issues with sugar. I love it. Sweets, chocolate, ice cream, puddings… you name it, I love it. Some would say I'm an addict.

The thing is, though, that my body can't tolerate too much of it, so when I've been on a sugar binge (usually when I'm on my last legs energetically) my mouth breaks out in ulcers. Those ulcers are telling me that what I'm putting in my mouth is hurting me. So I cut down on sugar for a while and the ulcers go away.

Until the next time.

Applying the 'how you do anything is how you do everything' principle, you'll see that my sugar issue is reflective of a much larger issue: that of how I treat my body and manage my health and try to keep burnout at bay (or not).

I love my work. It's my passion, my mission, my gift and my pleasure all in one package. But, again, my physical, spiritual and emotional body can't tolerate too much of it, so when – as often happens – I move into overdrive and start to do more than I can healthily manage, my body tells me to stop hurting myself. I get tired. I grind my teeth. My stomach gets sore. I get headaches. My throat hurts. My mouth gets ulcers from all the sugar.

In this way, I flirt with burnout. Sometimes I even go on a few dates with burnout, just to check whether it really is that bad for me. And, yes, it really is that bad for me. So I slow down, get more rest, stop taking on so much and feel better.

Until the next time.

You'd think that after so many years of dealing with these same issues, I'd have learned how to manage myself better. But, as my body tells me, my ability to self-regulate clearly needs some more work. Burnout management is, I think, a lifelong lesson for me.

BREAK A BAD HABIT

Habits can be good friends or terrible friends. Habits make us put on our seatbelts, brush our teeth before bed and wash our hands after we've used the loo. But habits can also make us mindlessly eat a bar of chocolate when we're tired, or eat lunch in front of our computers or read text messages while we're driving.

What are some of your bad habits? At home, at work, in private, in public; what are some of the things you habitually do that are bad for you?

Choose one, any one. Think about it, examine it, really engage with it. Then think about why you want to stop or change it.

* When are you more likely to do/think this thing? (For example, in my case, I eat more sugar when I'm tired, bored, hormonal or cold.)

* Is there a person or people that you're more likely to do this thing with or for? (For me, I tend to eat more sweets when I'm on my own.)

* Why do you think you think this/do this? What are you trying to tell yourself? (When I eat too much sugar it's because I'm tired or bored and starting to get physically, mentally or emotionally overwhelmed; the sugar craving is my body telling me that my energy is depleted.)

* Can you identify an early-warning system for yourself that helps you to be more aware of when you're in danger of doing/thinking this thing? (When I'm tired, bored, cold or hormonal I need to be on guard.)

* Can you come up with an alternative thought/action that's better for you? (I could have a bath, take a nap, go for a walk, take on less… and I can allow myself a reasonable amount of sugar so that I don't feel deprived and then go on a binge in retaliation against myself if I try to stop it altogether!)

BE HERE NOW

As you read this, are you fully, entirely and 100% present wherever you are and in whatever you're doing? Or are you worrying about something that may or may not be happening in another sphere of your life?

Everyone has a full and complex life, and the rest of your life doesn't stop just because you're at work (or at home or on a date or having a massage). Your family stresses don't disappear, your financial worries don't evaporate, your concerns about politics and the economy all continue to exist when you're at work. Worries about a report, a presentation or a meeting may enter uninvited when you're spending time with your family and friends. This is natural and understandable.

But it isn't desirable because when you're doing one thing but thinking about another, or being in one place but wishing you were somewhere else, you're neither here nor there; neither present nor absent. You're not doing justice to where you are when you're thinking about somewhere else. It doesn't matter if you're at work, at home, in the shopping centre or at a movie, if you aren't being fully present then you aren't really there.

Set true goals to leave burnout behind

If you want to make meaningful changes and set achievable goals in leaving burnout behind, you need to choose changes that you really do – truly, madly, deeply – want to achieve, rather than setting goals that you think you should want to achieve.

I've developed a 5-step process to help my clients to set and achieve goals and changes in order to lead a happier, healthier and burnout-free life. I call it *true* goal setting, and it's designed to help you achieve goals that are **t**angible, that are **r**ight for you, that you're **u**nambivalent about, and that are aligned with your **e**ssential self.

1. WHERE DO YOU NEED TO MAKE CHANGES IN YOUR LIFE?

I'm sure that while you were reading this book, you were thinking about things that you'd like to do differently – strengthening your boundaries, becoming less others-centred, saying no, asking for help, doing things that bring you more joy, or all of the above (hopefully all of the above and more), and I'm sure you already have some ideas about how to look after yourself better.

Now, write them all down. It may be useful to refer back to your wheel of life, and write down:

* Everything to do with your *work*
* Your attention to your own *personal growth and creativity*
* Your *physical environment* and what impact it's having on you
* How you feel about your *intimate relationship* status
* Your relationship with your *family and friends*
* How you feel about *money*
* Your ability to make and honour *'me' time*
* Everything to do with your *health*

Now set some goals. Think about each of these life areas in as much detail as possible (for example, work includes colleagues, physical space, salary, potential for growth and promotion, organisational culture…), then identify one or two goals for each area that you're feeling most overwhelmed in and by.

2. DISCARD THE SOCIAL-SELF GOALS

Our three selves exist to serve us. Our Survivor Self helps us feel and stay safe, while our essential self encourages us to follow our bliss. Our social self (or false self), which wants to make and keep other people happy, is primarily concerned with our being loved, accepted and approved of, and it warns us not to alienate the people we love. When these three selves work together and cooperate, bliss does indeed follow. But, as is more often the case, when the fear of alienating or disappointing those we love gets too large, we find ourselves compromising and doing things that often feel decidedly unblissful to us.

Goal-setting and achievement is often a battle of wills between our social and essential selves. We take on activities or responsibilities that we have no interest in or affinity for. We don't take on activities or responsibilities that we have great interest in and affinity for. We say yes when we want to say no, and no when we want to say yes. We resolve to wear lipstick every day even though makeup causes us to look and feel silly and brings us out in a rash. We join the gym even though being in an artificially lit and airconditioned environment gives us a headache. We turn down the opportunity to sing in a band for fear of what our family and friends would think.

When we allow our social self to set our goals, our essential self has to come to our rescue by making it hard (or impossible) for us to achieve those resolutions.

Think about all the things you've ever been encouraged or decided to do. Starting as far back as you can remember, make a note of all the hobbies you've ever spent your time, energy and attention on. Which of those did you enjoy so much that you chose to continue with them? I'm prepared to bet good money that the only activities that you enjoyed doing and found meaningful enough to choose to continue with were and are in alignment with your essential self.

Essential-self goals and social-self goals aren't mutually exclusive; in fact, the ideal goals and resolutions to set for ourselves are ones that find the balance between our essential and social selves.

Listen to your selves. Look at the list of goals you've identified and, being brutally honest with yourself, identify which are social-self goals and which are essential-self goals. Which goals are there for you and your own happiness and fulfilment, and which are there to keep other people happy? Draw a line through all the social-self goals, and underline all the essential-self goals.

3. SAY YES TO YOU

Earlier in the book, we discussed others-centredness and how it often means that we spend all our waking moments thinking about others, listening to others and doing things for others. Sometimes, it's only in the calm and quiet that descends when everyone else is asleep that we find the space to think about and remember our own needs and wants.

In our others-centredness we may decide on resolutions or goals that we aren't all that committed to, but that we think will make others happy. We may sign up for a cycle race because our partner loves cycling – even though we find it terrifying and horrible. Perhaps we register for a degree or course because we know it'll make our parents happy, even though we'd prefer to be doing something very different with our lives. Or maybe we agree to stop eating carbs (even though we love them, and they make us happy) to keep our friend company on their diet.

There may be many reasons we feel the need to pursue a goal that's others-centred. Whatever the reasons may be, if we agree to do something to keep others happy, there's less incentive for us to follow through with it. Or, even more troubling, we may achieve that goal – but we may do it at the expense of our own happiness.

Set your own goals. Look at your list of underlined goals and think about whether any of them may be others-centred. Goal by goal, ask yourself if each one is yours – something that you're truly, deeply committed to and excited about achieving – or if it's a goal that you've agreed to in order to keep someone else happy. If it's the latter, cross it out.

4. LOSE THE AMBIVALENCE

I believe that ambivalence is one of the biggest obstacles to progress. It stops us from meeting our goals because it keeps us from going after them with 100% of our energy, enthusiasm and will. I think that a lot of the time we're ambivalent about the goals we identify for ourselves, it's because they're not essential-self goals, or they're ones arising from others-centredness, so we rescue ourselves from achieving them by getting in our own way.

To be ambivalent is to be uncertain, to have a desire to say or do two opposite or conflicting things at the same time. When we're ambivalent about something, we have mixed feelings: we want it, but we don't; we aspire to achieve it, but we fear what will happen if we do. Or we want to get something, but the act of getting it is scary or off-putting to us.

Many of my clients come for coaching because they're frustrated about not reaching goals they've set themselves. On reflection, they've often been ambivalent about these goals. For example, wanting to be in a romantic relationship but not wanting to lose their independence, or wanting a salaried job but not wanting to give up too much time and energy for creative pursuits, or wanting to be seen but not wanting to become too visible, or wanting to be fit and healthy but hating gym and organised exercise, or wanting to be busy and in demand but not wanting to get burnout.

It's only when we're absolutely, unequivocally and unambivalently convinced that we'd like to achieve something that we make sure that we do so.

In talking about conquering Mount Everest, mountaineer WH Murray said, 'Until one is committed there is hesitancy, the chance to draw back, always ineffectiveness. [But] the moment one definitely commits oneself, then… all sorts of things occur to help one that would otherwise never have occurred. A whole stream of events issues from the decision, raising in one's favour all manner of incidents and meetings and material assistance which no man would have believed would have come his way.'

Be 100% certain. Revisit your list of goals. Is there anything on it that you have mixed feelings about? Maybe you want to run a marathon but don't have the physical stamina right now? Or you want to start cooking organic vegan meals every night but don't have the emotional or physical wherewithal to make that happen just yet? Being brutally honest with yourself, select only the goals that you're unambivalent about and absolutely convinced that you'll be able to achieve.

5. SET TRUE GOALS

You've assessed all your goals and identified the ones that don't truly serve you or reflect your own priorities and desires. Now it's time to identify one or two – three at the most – *true* goals for yourself. And remember, each tiny choice you make leads to the big changes you desire in your life.

You're likely to have more success with achieving just a few small *true* goals than you are striving to achieve a whole lot of untrue ones. If you can start to change the tiny problems, the larger ones will start to change too. You can add new goals once you have the first couple up and running and they're not requiring so much effort to make happen any more. Again, set yourself up to succeed, not fail.

Plan for success. Make sure your goals are:

Tangible – be clear about what you're going to do, where, when and how.

Right for you – the goals must have meaning for you, rather than feeling important for others.

Unambivalent – you must have no mixed feelings about the goals themselves, or your ability to achieve them.

Essential-self aligned – the goals must reflect the desires of your essential self rather than your social self.

REACH YOUR OWN *TRUE* GOALS

Identify two or three *true* goals, and create a plan to achieve each one:

❋ Why do you want to achieve it?

❋ How will you go about achieving it?

❋ Who (if anyone) will you need to ask for help in achieving it?

❋ What (if anything) will you need to say no to in order to achieve it?

❋ When would you like to achieve it by?

Help yourself by...

Rome wasn't built in a day, and neither will new habits and responses be. Be patient in your quest to regain and maintain your energy and enthusiasm for life. To get on the road to recovery and rejuvenation, you need to make looking after and taking care of yourself as habitual as looking after others has been for you.

Be kind to yourself. When you're setting goals or identifying new or different ways of being, show yourself compassion and kindness. Set kind goals – the sort of goals that are meaningful to you and that you may actually have a snowball's chance in hell of achieving – and show yourself compassion if and when you don't do as well as you'd hoped.

Stop the self-sabotage. Identify ways that you can take better care of yourself, rather than pushing yourself too hard or expecting too much of yourself.

Say no/ask for help. You can't do it all, even if you want to. If you haven't already done this, get cracking immediately with identifying what's not working for you any more and say no to it. Ask for help wherever you can – remember that letting people help you is letting them love you. And saying no to things that don't serve you is helping (and loving) yourself.

Be mindful. In order to know what you need, to identify what you can say no to or ask for help with, and to practise compassion, you must be mindful. And in order to be mindful, you must create the time and space required to connect with yourself and your needs and wants. Find time every day to get still and quiet and turn inwards. Learn to listen to yourself.

WHAT HAVE YOU GOT TO BE GRATEFUL FOR?

It's so easy to get into a poor-me, everyone-else-has-it-easy-and-I-have-it-so-hard frame of mind. We can so quickly slip into 'compare and despair' thinking, where we convince ourselves that everyone (or at least someone) else is having a better time than we are, especially when we're tired and stressed.

Bear in mind that whatever we appreciate, appreciates – in other words, what we choose to put our attention on gets bigger and more important in our minds. If we pay attention to negative, disappointing events, they'll become more negative and more disappointing. Similarly, if we choose to pay attention to positive and uplifting things, we become aware of more and more positive and uplifting things around us.

Identify five things that you're grateful for right now. Big or small, transient or permanent – blue skies, rain, running water, indoor plumbing, a full stomach, delicious coffee, an uplifting conversation, a recent promotion, family and friends – you'll always be able to find things to appreciate.

And there's nothing like consciously identifying what we have to be grateful for to enable us to be happier and appreciate all that we have.

Moving forward, burnout free

If you've ever had a stomach ulcer you'll know that, without treating your stomach correctly moving forward, there's a good chance that the ulcer will return. There is and always will be a weak spot in your gastric lining that will be vulnerable to relapse.

Burnout is the same. It leaves a scar on our physical and emotional bodies – a scar that can easily be exposed to reveal an open wound.

In order to stay passionate, productive and purposeful, we need to be mindful and vigilant about protecting our boundaries, doing the right things and remembering to look after ourselves. My hope is that this book will help you to do that. The practical tips should assist with better self-care, and the soul-searching tools should help you to understand how you push yourself too far and to change that. I hope these tips and tools will help you to not only heal your burnout, but also to regain and maintain your purpose, passion and productivity in a sustained and sustainable way.

A DAILY TOOL FOR RECOVERY

Burnout is a complex disease and it requires a comprehensive approach to recovery, something that doesn't always feel so easy when we're overwhelmed and overstretched. That's why I've condensed everything we've worked through already into a handy little tool I like to call the Spanner.

The Spanner is a 7-step process designed to build on all the work you've done so far and to develop a simple yet powerful daily practice that will help you to not only regain but maintain your life force. It takes all the information and tasks that have been presented in this book and captures them in a simple and easy-to-use format.

S is for Self. We get burnout when we stop thinking about ourselves, when we put ourselves last, and when we stop listening and responding to what our bodies are telling us about ourselves. We need to reconnect with ourselves and our spirits by practising self-care, self-love and self-compassion, and by remembering who we are and what's important to us.

P is for Peace and quiet. If you want to recover from burnout, you need to learn (or relearn) to connect with your body, mind and spirit. You need to slow down and find some peace and quiet in your day. Ideally, we need 20 minutes a day to be quiet: to rest, relax, meditate, journal, sleep … whatever you do with your 20 minutes, make them count by making sure the only person you talk or listen to is yourself. If 20 uninterrupted minutes feels too scary or too impossible, you could start with 5 minutes and work your way up to 20. You could also make it easier for yourself by going for a gentle (solo) walk, or even driving your car with the radio and music switched off – when we're walking or driving in silence, we're able to connect with ourselves without feeling as though we're wasting time.

A is for Ask and Accept and Allow. You make your life much easier when you allow yourself to ask for and to receive. It doesn't matter if it's help, love, advice, compliments, feedback or any other positive assistance, if you allow it in, you'll lighten your load. Letting people help you is letting people love you – and it's also letting you love yourself.

N is for No. Being overwhelmed is caused by having too many things on our plate, and doing too many of the things that aren't right for us leads to burnout. We need to be very mindful about what we say yes to and what we say no to. Every day, think about everything that's expected of you (by yourself or by others) and choose what you can say no to. You can start small (saying no to staying up late, to eating chocolate instead of making a healthy meal, to the dog begging for more food) and work your way up to more difficult refusals (saying no to a social invitation, to a bad relationship, to a promotion that will make you unhappy). Say yes to you by saying no to what isn't serving you.

N is also for Nourish. One of the first and most obvious signs of burnout is a craving for sugar, carbohydrates, caffeine and salt. And the more carbs and caffeine we consume, the more we want; and the more tired we get, the less energy we have to make proper, healthy food. And, of course, when we're feeling tired and overwhelmed, we want to treat ourselves to nice, comforting, carby food – so much more consoling than vegetables and salad. But that comforting food is the very last thing your body needs. What it needs is food that's fresh and high in protein, and vitamins and minerals to build itself back up. Nourish your body, mind and soul by eating nourishing food, thinking nourishing thoughts and doing nourishing things with people who feed your soul.

E is for Exercise. Burnout drains us of vitality and enthusiasm. What little energy we do have is spent holding ourselves together and getting through the day. All we want to do is go home and collapse in front of some mindless TV series while we eat chocolate and chips. The last thing we feel like doing is hitting the gym and working up a sweat – which is why I don't recommend this to my clients. What's very helpful, however, is doing some gentle exercise every day: a walk, a soothing yoga class, jumping on your kids' trampoline for a few minutes – these are all the kinds of exercise that gradually and compassionately let oxygen in and stress out. They release adrenaline and get the blood moving. Gentle exercise helps you sleep better while improving your appetite for healthy food.

R is for Recharge. We can only recover from burnout when we learn how to recharge all the areas of our lives. Physically we recharge by sleeping, by moving gently and by eating healthy food. Mentally we recharge by thinking less and feeling more, and by giving our brains a break. Emotionally we recharge by listening to what our emotions are telling us – and by responding to them appropriately. Spiritually we recharge by reconnecting with ourselves and our own spirit. And we recharge relationally and restore our sense of belonging by reinvesting in the relationships that nourish us – by paying them the time, attention and effort that they (and we) deserve.

These steps aren't mutually exclusive, so please don't feel put off them by thinking that doing 7 things every day will be too much. For instance, you can have a 20-minute silent walk by yourself every morning to plan your day. You can use the check-in tool to identify what you're feeling and what you're needing and what your agenda needs to be for the day. You can identify who to ask for help from, and what to say no to. You can plan your nourishing meals for the day. You can think about who you'd like to reach out to during the day in order to maintain your relationships. And you can do all of this while getting some gentle exercise.

When you're able to use your Spanner every day, you'll soon start to feel happier, more energised and more connected to yourself. When you internalise the Spanner, you'll also be able to look after yourself better now and as you move forward in your burnout-free life.

WRITE IT DOWN

Your brain is a busy place. In the foreground is whatever you're thinking about right now, while the background is filled (often to overflowing) with many and varied thoughts, such as what you want to say in the meeting you're about to attend, how the last conversation went, making a mental note to follow up on that email that came in yesterday, what to eat for lunch, what to make for supper, when to squeeze in a trip to the bathroom...

Your brain is like a 24-hour TV news channel that's constantly playing at low volume in the background. It's important to turn off the constant news stream so that you can rest, relax and refocus. You can do this by picking up a pen and paper and writing. Writing is a simple, effective and cheap way to turn off your internal TV by getting what's in your head onto paper.

Try it now. Just five minutes (or more if you can) of writing will help you feel more in control of your thoughts and emotions. It doesn't matter if it's a to-do list, a to-don't list, free-writing about fears and feelings, mind-mapping reports and strategies, reminiscing, planning, or dreaming and scheming, you can put it down by writing it down.